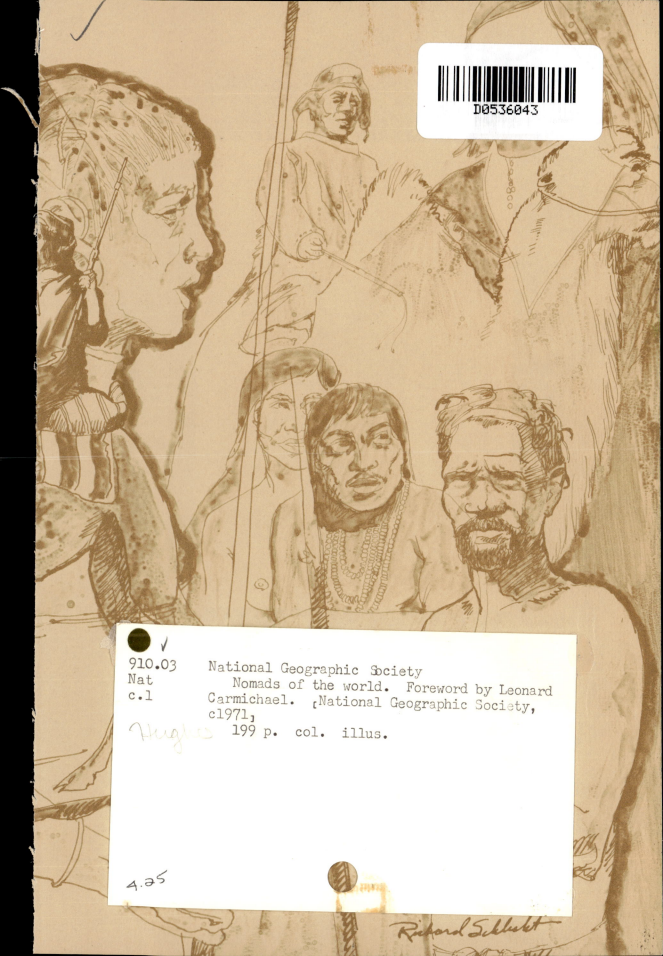

D0536043

910.03   National Geographic Society
Nat   Nomads of the world. Foreword by Leonard
c.1   Carmichael. [National Geographic Society,
         c1971]
Hughes   199 p. col. illus.

4.25

Richard Schlecht

BEULAH B. HUGHES
GEOGRAPHY COLLECTION

YOLO COUNTY LIBRARY
DAVIS BRANCH

NOMADS
of the World

Prepared by the Special Publications Division,
ROBERT L. BREEDEN, Chief

Foreword by LEONARD CARMICHAEL,
Vice President for Research and Exploration,
National Geographic Society, Washington, D. C.
MELVIN M. PAYNE, President
MELVILLE BELL GROSVENOR, Editor-in-Chief
GILBERT M. GROSVENOR, Editor

YOLO COUNTY FREE LIBRARY
WOODLAND - CALIFORNIA

910.03
Nat
C.1

Nomads of the World

Published by

The National Geographic Society
Melvin M. Payne, *President*
Melville Bell Grosvenor, *Editor-in-Chief*
Gilbert M. Grosvenor, *Editor*
Andrew H. Brown, *Consulting Editor*

Contributing Authors

Mohammad Bahmanbegui, Donald P. Cole,
  Alyette de Munck, Neville Dyson-Hudson,
  Victor Englebert, Loren McIntyre,
  H. Arlo Nimmo, Satya Pal Ruhela

Prepared by

The Special Publications Division
Robert L. Breeden, *Editor*
Donald J. Crump, *Associate Editor*
Philip B. Silcott, *Senior Assistant Editor*
Mary Ann Harrell, *Manuscript Editor*
Cynthia Russ Ramsay, Tee Loftin Snell,
  Assistants to the Editor
Ann H. Crouch, Linda Lu Moore,
  Nancy B. Zucker, *Researchers*

Illustrations

William L. Allen, *Picture Editor*
Josephine B. Bolt, William R. Gray, Jr.,
  H. Robert Morrison, Tee Loftin Snell,
  Elizabeth C. Wagner, *Picture Legends*

Layout and Design

Joseph A. Taney, *Art Director*
Josephine B. Bolt, *Associate Art Director*
Ursula Perrin, *Design Assistant*
Betty Cloninger, John D. Garst, Jr.,
  Nancy Schweickart, Monica Woodbridge,
  Map Research and Production

Production and Printing

Robert W. Messer, *Production Manager*
Margaret Murin Skekel, *Production Assistant*
James R. Whitney, John R. Metcalfe,
  Engraving and Printing
Marta I. Bernal, Suzanne J. Jacobson,
  Elizabeth Van Beuren Joy, Raja D. Mur-
  shed, Donna Rey Naame, Joan Perry,
  Suzanne B. Thompson, *Staff Assistants*
Jolene McCoy, *Index*

Copyright © 1971 National Geographic Society. All rights reserved. Reproduction of the whole or any part of the contents without written permission is prohibited.
Standard Book Number 87044-098-5
Library of Congress Catalog Card Number 78-151946

OVERLEAF PHOTOGRAPH, ROLAND MICHAUD; ENDSHEET ART,
RICHARD SCHLECHT; BOOKBINDING, JOSEPHINE B. BOLT

VICTOR ENGLEBERT (BELOW AND PAGE 1)

Mimicking her veiled father, a Tuareg girl of the Sahara hides her nose and mouth. By custom, men always wear veils; women screen their faces with headcloths for travel or before strangers and in-laws. Wide-ranging nomads, the Tuareg take camel caravans through a land of no roads. Overleaf: On a gravel-strewn highland in the Zāgros Mountains of Iran, a Qashqā'ī family moves to winter pasture near the Persian Gulf. Their flocks of goats and sheep move before them. Page 1: Bororo youngsters of Niger carry goatskin water bags slung beneath their donkeys.

Foreword

Anyone who leads a reasonably settled life—as most of us do—finds a special appeal in the thought of far journeys and a life of travel. Indeed, the strength of this appeal suggests something deep-rooted in our nature. C. G. Jung, certainly one of the most original thinkers of our time, wrote much about archetypes, or modes of thought and behavior present in all of us and derived from the ancient races whose descendants we are. Many scholars dismiss this concept as unproved. But certain modes of thought and action can seem so fascinating and so compelling that they have an almost mystical and intrusive power in our lives. For many people, the idea of nomadism has just this kind of inner, unexplained, dynamic force. It is a rare person who can honestly say that he has not sometimes had an almost irresistible desire to pull up stakes and move on.

In our own culture we see people who move on with marked frequency. Freedom to travel is one of our most prized rights. As this book makes clear, we share a value cherished by nomadic tribes—and by societies we might not consider nomadic at all. The Germans have a word, *Wanderjahre,* for years of travel considered as a proper climax to a thorough education. They also speak of *Wanderleben,* a roving life in which one follows his *Wanderlust,* or the siren call of the road.

These examples should remind us that the nomadic life takes many forms. Of the great variety of nomadic peoples in the world today, this book can present only a sample. Yet it describes them well and vividly, and shows that they have good reason for their travels. Often they move in response to changes of environment.

In recent years, scientists have actively studied the causes of yearly migration of mammals, birds, and fish such as salmon. These studies also illuminate the movements of people who live by hunting and gathering food. Thus an annual rainy season brings changes in grasses and shrubs; herbivorous animals move to feed on these plants; and hunters follow them. If a herding life supersedes hunting, men move according to a similar cycle to lead their animals at the proper seasons to new pastures. Comparable cycles marked the life of many American Indian tribes, who would journey to rivers to catch fish that return from the oceans each year to spawn.

Annual cyclic changes of the hormone balance in animals—often cued by temperature and changes in the duration of daylight—have long determined the internal biological clocks that are basic in releasing inborn migration patterns. The modern Scandinavians who seek the sunny shores of the Mediterranean on a winter holiday, or retired residents of Maine or Montana who go to Florida in January, are fitting their lives into an age-old pattern. Goethe, who had felt the chill of north European winds, knew this when he wrote: "Know you the land where the lemon-trees bloom? . . . There, there I would go. . . ."

So an ancient appeal motivates not only the nomads who figure in this book, but also the modern city-dweller as he turns his car for a Saturday outing on the open road. The reader may find that he understands more of himself and also of his fellow men as he turns the pages.

Your Society takes pleasure in presenting this book, which combines the insight of professional anthropologists and the sensitive interest of nonprofessional observers. We hope that each reader will find in it great pleasure, a new perspective on his own experience, and a new respect for the varied life patterns of the peoples of our world.

Leonard Carmichael

Contents

Pausing in their wanderings, Gaduliya Lohars sing Hindu songs for fairgoers at Lamana, India. Finger cymbals and a harmonium accompany them.

NATIONAL GEOGRAPHIC PHOTOGRAPHER GEORGE F. MOBLEY

Lush green grass—the goal of all wandering herders—feeds the flocks of Bakhtiari tribesmen. Today as in past

Inheriting — and Extending — Man's Nomads Find Freedom and Identity

By NEVILLE DYSON-HUDSON, *D. Phil.*

ANTHONY HOWARTH

generations they rely for summer grazing on their high alpine meadows among the Zāgros Mountains of Iran.

Oldest Technique of Survival,

in the Life They Follow

SPEAR IN HAND, the wizened old man lifted himself from a tiny wooden stool and stepped within the leafy branches that marked out the ground as a place of sacrifice. Looking into the faces of the men seated around, he lifted his spear and called: "Cattle, are there not cattle?" "There are!" roared his audience. "The cattle of the Karimojong, are they not here?" "They are!" shouted the people. "And will they not become fat, these cattle?" he continued. Again came the roar of response: "They are fat!"

As the prayer leader chanted his questions and the adults answered in chorus, I struggled to follow this litany which blessed the herds and people of the Karimojong in northeast Uganda. Fifteen years ago, it was my first field trip. That ritual gave me my first opportunity to see how these people introduce into all the important events of life some symbol of the animals that enable them to survive in one of the harsh places of the earth. It was my first experience of the intense absorption with livestock that marks pastoral nomads.

This absorption—a combination of deep knowledge and emotional concern—outsiders often find hard to understand. But it accounts for the success of nomads in keeping animals alive in areas where, for all our technology, we could not. It partly accounts for their preference to live off milk products and blood rather than meat; men are reluctant to kill animals they know so well except when the requirements of hospitality or religion turn the act of destruction into gift or sacrifice. Often such people consider cattle as morally conscious creatures made happy by their owner's achievements, or likely to gore him or withhold their milk if they are angry at his wrongdoing.

Anthropologists sometimes see the world too much in terms of their own field experiences. I find that I am doing that now, because not all nomads are herders. Rather, nomads are people who rely on movement to survive, and this movement leaves recognizable marks on their culture and form of society. But nomadic life takes many forms, because there are many ways of surviving on the move.

People may carry their skills and weapons with them, and so survive on the move by hunting—like the Akuriyos of Surinam, the Bushmen of the Kalahari, and the Aboriginal Australians. They may carry their tools and products as they move, and so survive by trading or offering services, as with the Lohars or Gypsies. They can carry their food on the hoof and be herders, like the Lapps and the Mongols. I think it reasonable to speak of nomadic farmers, technically called shifting cultivators, when people rotate not their crops but their fields and themselves. Thus the Iban of Sarawak may spend 20 years in cyclic movement over a periodically cleared and cultivated territory. In fact, pinning nomads down by a definition can be every bit as difficult as finding them when you are in the field.

This problem of definition—just the kind of thing that gets anthropologists cross with each other at scientific meetings—we inherited.

Painted with designs suggesting clouds and rain, an Aboriginal Australian holds his spear and spear-thrower, sophisticated weapons of a primordial way of life. Hunting and gathering food in the western deserts, men like these wandered the territories of their tribes, finding deep spiritual significance in scattered water holes and landmarks of timeless rock.

ROBERT B. GOODMAN

For 15 years NEVILLE DYSON-HUDSON *of the Johns Hopkins University has studied human ecology in nomadic societies with his biologist wife Rada.*

Each spring the climb begins, 150 miles over steep slopes and high passes to sardsir—cool summer pastures—of the Bakhtiari. Like other Iranian tribes, they hold long-standing rights to specific areas. Felt-capped men ford icy mountain streams carrying kids, lambs, and children, or float them across on goatskin rafts. Coaxing their flocks up and down sheer rock faces, followed by long-skirted women with cradles strapped on their backs, the Bakhtiari struggle over the rugged terrain. With autumn they return to garmsir, the warm places. Below, stone lions mark graves of brave men, heroes of the tribe's warlike past; mares and colts memorialize their wealth and power.

ANTHONY HOWARTH

Age-old routine—setting up camp (above), breaking it again, moving on to new grass—faltered in 1971 for Afghan kuchi, nomads. They stayed all year in winter pasture, their sheep facing starvation, as drought flayed valleys in the Hindu Kush. Custom secures land for their use, while the Yörük of Turkey (below) must bargain with landlords each season for

THOMAS J. ABERCROMBIE, NATIONAL GEOGRAPHIC STAFF (TOP); DR. DANIEL BATES

grazing. Roasting coffee, a Yörük mother rests before the next day's climb to yayla, *summer camp in the Taurus range.*

Some of our labels come from the turn of the century when anthropologists were mainly interested in the evolution of Western civilization. They found it convenient to imagine "stages" of social development. They happily arranged the world's societies into sequences, as if inspecting so many living fossils, and clearly considered their categories as natural as species of plants and animals. When we talk of "hunting societies," "pastoral societies," or "agricultural societies," we are using old labels of this sort.

These labels can mislead us. Anthropologists don't actually observe societies (though we talk as if we did). We observe populations—sets of people—and populations show an interesting determination to survive however they can, despite the label some scholar may have pinned to them. Take the Karimojong I knew as herders, for instance. They lost almost all their cattle to disease and drought about 80 years ago, and to stay alive they took to hunting elephant for meat. Eventually they found they could exchange the otherwise useless tusks for cattle from visiting traders, and within a generation were back in the cattle business again. Such flexibility is common with humans, but our professional labels don't often reflect it, and anthropologists can still look unhappy if one mixes up these economic "types."

To be fair, our problem in defining nomads arises from more than old labels. In the 1930's my profession somewhat self-consciously set about becoming a science, rather than an inventory of odd customs. It announced its intention to search for universal laws explaining human societies. But this is difficult unless you keep the factors you deal with limited in number and under strict control.

So we might, for instance, feel we can reach interesting and reliable generalizations about hunters. Typically they live in loosely organized small bands, thinly scattered; their patterns of work vary with age and sex, not as specialized occupations—and so on. But lumping hunters, herders, wandering traders, and shifting cultivators together as "nomads" soon makes us despair of being able to say anything useful. There seem to be far too many variables.

This professional caution, based as it is on hard work, deserves respect; but it can cost us a lot. If we consider societies which have movement for survival in common, though not much else, we immediately face questions that concern us all. Right away we see that "survival" means more than material things, for a people may move—as in the Book of Exodus—to find freedom or purity as well as game or pastures. Indeed, nomadic groups have regularly been in trouble with political authorities for the one reason as much as for the other. Driven by the needs of their herds, they may move to new pasture, whoever owns it; driven by needs less tangible but no less urgent, they may move from unwanted change or unreasonable control, whoever brings it.

Indeed freedom, for an individual as well as for a group, ranks high among nomad values. It may be the freedom of an adult man to take the group for which he is responsible to wherever he thinks it will survive best. It may be the freedom to make and break alliances as he sees fit, constrained only by his allegiance to the group for which he is responsible and to the society from which he draws his own rights. Working with the Karimojong, the Turkana of Kenya, the Bisharin of Sudan, I have found this freedom in varying forms—and always found it attractive. I would expect to find it in any nomadic society.

Among nomads, too, "freedom" raises the question that has long fascinated political philosophers, and citizens who vote, in the societies of the West: What is the right relationship between individual freedom and obligation to the political society that guarantees it?

More clearly, perhaps, than the rest of us, nomads see that freedom to make decisions goes step for step with accountability. They live, often, in a rigorous world where the margin of survival stretches very thin. Wrong decisions easily lead to disaster. The nomadic groups we see are the successful ones. The unsuccessful joined the sands of the desert, the litter of the forest, or the barren ground of the tundra long ago. In asserting the right to move at will, nomads often claim no more and no less than their right to survive.

If we think mainly about movement, we also see that nomads abound in our own society, and wonder whether the problems that nomads face are really so strange after all. Commuters who live in Connecticut but survive by exploiting resources in New York City follow a path as regular and distinctive as any Persian nomad on his migratory tribal road. Their concern about the unpredictability of suburban railroads fills just as much conversation as some other nomad's concern about the unpredictable movements of rain or game. A commercial traveler for the garment industry may be separated by only one significant variable (household location) from a Gypsy, who also survives by putting his skills and his products on the road.

Officers and their families in the U. S. Foreign Service may run a cycle not too different from shifting cultivators. The migrant laborers on whom so much American agriculture depends are as ignored and distrusted by the settled groups through which they pass as any nomadic group elsewhere. And what of the family life of those nomadic households who move from one trailer park to another across America as their men build roads, or whose concessions for hot-dog stands take them from one state fair to another in an annual round?

We should not really be surprised to find so many forms of nomadic life. For much of human history—even in hominid times—we have evidence of populations surviving by movement rather than in permanently settled communities. Olduvai Gorge in East Africa has yielded signs of transient settlement 1,800,000 years ago. At Torralba and Ambrona, in the limestone valleys of Spain, humans repeatedly gathered 300,000 years ago to hunt and butcher animals that migrated through the mountain passes.

By contrast, when we speak of animal domestication we speak of relatively recent events: say 10,000 years for sheep and goats, at least 6,000 for cattle, and perhaps 3,500 years for camels. Separating the sometimes muddled notions of nomadism and pastoralism, then, has the advantage of reminding us that the nomadic way of life is an ancient as well as a persistent human experience. (Continued on page 23)

JOHN EARLE (BELOW); CLAUDE W. LEAVITT

Hunched near a smoldering fire in the forests of Surinam, Tiramu (opposite), son of the leader of an Akuriyo Indian band, arranges bamboo arrowtips—to be poisoned with curare—on a drying rack. Discovered by missionaries in 1968, the fewscore Akuriyos travel in groups of 10 to 25, moving as they deplete the game, fruit, nuts, and wild honey—or as spirits warn them. Chacon (above), one of the last pure-blooded Yahgan Indians, stands outside her home in Tierra del Fuego. Nomadic fishers, her people survived in a remote, bleak land until decimated by epidemic diseases contracted from Europeans.

Earth and sky merge into a monochromatic void (below) as Lapp nomads take a train of reindeer and sleds across a snowbound vidda—plateau—in Norway. Some 5,000 Lapps still herd reindeer, traversing the frigid wastes of northern Scandinavia in seasonal moves to pasture. During a hundred-mile, month-long migration to summer grazing, a family melts snow to make coffee and lunches off dried reindeer meat with bread and butter. They stop to eat and rest when the herd of 1,500 finds forage; otherwise the trek continues, for the deer lead the way. At right, a Lapp and his dog doze on a rock. A skier scans the horizon for strays.

NATIONAL GEOGRAPHIC PHOTOGRAPHER GEORGE F. MOBLEY

Descendants of Genghis Khan's world-famous warriors, sturdy herdsmen of the Mongolian People's Republic lasso horses with an urga, *a pole with a rope noose at the end. Mongol nomads prize their hardy small horses not only for mobility but also as emblems of wealth. For everyday sustenance, they keep sheep, cattle, camels, goats, and yaks. Each strain of stock thrives best on specific forage, and the experience of many generations has built up a lore of expert knowledge for the pastoral life. Although nomads now belong to collectives and the government encourages them to settle down as ranchers growing fodder and silage crops, herdsmen still move their animals in seasonal migrations. Their round felt tents, famous as* yurts *but called* gers *by their owners, provide shelter in mountains, steppes, and deserts. Far in the west, the Kazakhs—largest minority in the republic, pastoral nomads of Turkish origin —keep their own language and traditions. An elder (right) wears a fur-trimmed coat and fur hat with lappets to protect his ears: the dress of winter. Galloping his pony-size mount, a Kazakh carries a golden eagle, tamed to hunt small game and symbolic of manly valor.*

N.G.S. PHOTOGRAPHER DEAN CONGER (BELOW); GYORGY LAJOS © INTERFOTO MTI, HUNGARY

BERNARD HERMANN, GAMMA, PHOTOREPORTERS INC.
(ABOVE); GYORGY LAGOS © INTERFOTO MTI, HUNGARY

*Dwarfed by outcrops of
rock, light tents flank a
canvas-covered ger in
summer camp. Inside,
sunlight glistens on a cup
of fermented mare's milk
—the Mongol delicacy. A
woman paints a* toono, *the crown of a ger's
wooden frame.*

N.G.S. PHOTOGRAPHER DEAN CONGER (OPPOSITE)

Ancient, widespread, and varied as the nomadic life is, the forms shown in this book could nonetheless disappear in our lifetime, eliminated by fear, by shame, by greed, above all by ignorance.

Governments regard nomads warily; in remote and modern times alike, in Europe and in Asia and in Africa, they have been shaken when nomadic tribesmen moved against them. Ordinary people in settled communities, too, may long to possess empty land or fear the nomads who roam in it—as raiders come to loot a village, as forest hunters come to attack a mission station, as herders come to trample crops.

Yet millions of pastoral Fulani scattered across West Africa prove that nomads are not inevitably fierce and predatory, for they pass amicably among settled people and trade with them. Yörük shepherds in Turkey bargain peacefully for the use of pastures that settled villagers own. I believe East African cattle-herders to be threatened more by the expansionist desires of agricultural neighbors and international conservationists than they themselves threaten either group. And Elizabeth Marshall Thomas's term for the Bushmen of the Kalahari— "the Harmless People"—applies to many other hunters.

Nevertheless bureaucrats, who find nomads offensively untidy for their filing systems, often strengthen popular distrust. As new states set out to become strong modern nations, this bureaucratic irritation readily becomes official disapproval. Nomads who shun a part in the cash economy, who wear traditional clothing or none at all, who lack formal education, are considered as hindering the nation's development, as shaming it before outsiders. Discouraging, even abolishing, nomads becomes a patriotic urge; but it also destroys unique skills, a unique commitment, and so destroys a people's identity.

To grasp the mainsprings of social life, even the social scientist is forced back on his own experience. This may be why I view the commitment to nomadic life in terms of a personal experience among the Karimojong. It cannot explain the commitment of a Bajau seafarer in his narrow boat, or a wandering Lohar, or a Pygmy in the forest that is both father and mother to him. But it remains my particular touchstone for the nomad's readiness to celebrate the harsh places of the earth as if they were the finest, and to consider a perpetual struggle for survival as the best life of all.

Because adult Karimojong take their formal name from a favorite steer in their herd, I bought an animal from my missionary friend Bob Clark. In my new identity as Apalongoronyang—Father of the Roan Ox with the Tan Face—I seemed more accepted. My adoptive brother took my name-ox into his own herd, taught me how to care for it, how to decorate it with collar and bell, how (with salt) to make it come when I called. When it first came to me he was happy, because that was proper between a man and the ox of his identity. I had not mastered the language yet, so friends composed simple lyrics about it for me, and insisted I take my turn singing its praises at dances, as a man should for the ox which is his identity. And they taught me my battle cry, which contained my ox-name, so I could assert who I truly was when I needed my courage and charged my enemies.

23

The Karimojong call such an animal "a beloved ox"; mine became so for me. Then disease struck my brother's herd, killing cattle, among them my name-ox. I sat dejected when I heard the news, uncharitably certain that my brother would have been more watchful with his own animal. When neighbors came to sympathize, I thought only that they discerned this and were trying to rid me of unfair suspicion. But I was mistaken.

Day after day, men stopped in to see me. Some had walked 30 or 40 miles to do so. Their faces were concerned, their voices low, and always their remarks followed the same pattern.

"We are sad about your ox. We are very sad. It is a bad thing. The land is bad now. This land itself is bad. Did you hear that at such a place they have had sickness? It is very bad there. Did you hear that so-and-so has lost his cattle? Many of them. And so-and-so also, a bull that he liked. And so-and-so, he lost many cows. They say there is very little milk for his people now. It is a bad time this. The land is bad now. And your ox. That is a bad business. Everywhere now things seem bad."

Gradually I came to see that in this consolation they did me great kindness, for it is not unknown for a man to commit suicide at such a loss. They came to protect me, to emphasize that I was not uniquely the victim of misfortune, but only shared in the more general grief of the world; and this while painful was not unbearable.

In their kindness they revealed much of themselves. People feel such grief where they regard their animals as in some sense companions, tied to their own being—not merely as objects to be possessed and disposed of. Their commitment to herding springs from this sense of being-in-cattle, I believe. This merging of identities makes bearable an otherwise intolerable round of labor in harsh circumstances that, day in day out, begins long before dawn and ends long after dark—that leaves even the night hours to be spent stretched on a cowhide at a little fire by the corral, one ear open for sounds of unrest and danger. Bringing the herd back full after a long day's grazing, yourself empty-bellied and apprehensive of things which prey at night, you sing softly to the cattle of the hours you have shared, and so feel easier in your mind. For a small herdboy, shivering naked under a tree in a wet-season storm with rain cold on the skin, the chill is more endurable because cattle are life and not just labor to him.

If in our lifetime we suppress nomads, we shall have done by human harshness what natural harshness could not do. To abolish nomads because they have other skills, know other things, hold other aspirations, and live by other customs than ours—in short, because they are different—is as unwise as it is unworthy. Contemplating the prospect of settling Saharan nomads, a UNESCO symposium on the arid zone somberly noted that the world should not "let a region which feeds a million individuals return to the desert, at a time when a third of mankind is suffering from hunger."

There is a place for nomads in the world, often enough a place we cannot use without them. We must not steal it from them, for if we do, we reduce the richness of human life—we rob ourselves.

DR. PAUL SPENCER

Samburu women—of low status in a tribe ruled by its elders—dance "The
Ox," each soloist boasting of her favorite beast, arms mimicking its
horns. Cattle sustain these nomads in the scrub desert of northern Kenya.

Squatting by her reed-covered cart-home at the edge of the asphalt road entering Gangapur, a Gaduliya Lohar wif

Bullock-cart Blacksmiths, Gaduliya
LOHARS Bring Forges to Rajasthan

By Satya Pal Ruhela, Ph.D.
Illustrations by National Geographic Photographer George F. Mobley

serves breakfast. The family belongs to a group of wandering Hindu artisans numbering more than 25,000 people.

Villages

MY SEARCH for the sub-band of Nathu Gaduliya Lohar, a cart blacksmith whose religious songs I wanted to record, had led me to a dozen villages on the plains and green hills of Rajasthan in northwestern India. Nowhere had I found Nathu's massive cart-home and bullocks. I inquired for him by name—the caste or subcaste provides surnames among these artisans—without success. I had simply wasted a week looking for a man on the move. I decided to take the bus all the way back to the city of Ajmer and then to Mangliawas, a farming village 16 miles beyond, to see if my long-time friends Harji Gaduliya Lohar and his brother Gopi could tell me where Nathu might be camping.

By good fortune that only a few Lohars could ever expect, Harji and Gopi have escaped the worst level of poverty that imprisons these nomads—the elders of Mangliawas gave them the land of their old camping site. Each had built a one-room house of stone and brick, complete with porch of corrugated asbestos. They don't sleep, eat, or work indoors, but merely store their supplies and valuables there. Harji once told me some members of his family still have the nomad's fear that the roof might suddenly collapse and injure them—"even though I made this roof good and strong myself." I knew they would be just outside, easy for me to find.

Even if I had not known the site, I could have gone straight to it from the bus stop. All I had to do was walk toward the slow, rhythmic pounding of their sledgehammer. Thud...thud...thud....

Despite having seen these artisan nomads at work many times during the 11 years I have studied them, I still find the scene rather startling, mostly because the person swinging the long-handled hammer, or *ghan*, is usually a woman.

In her long skirt of brightly printed cotton, her red and green *kanchali*, or brassiere, and her light *odhani*, yards of gaudy cloth draped loosely about her, she stands barefoot before the little anvil, the *eran*. Over her shoulder she raises the great hammer and brings it smashing down. Again and again she strikes. Thud! Thud! She hits the ten-pound hammerhead against a scrap of fire-hot iron her husband holds with tongs on the anvil. Her 46 ivory—or plastic—bracelets, irremovable symbols of marriage, jangle and click with each blow.

Slender, barely five feet tall, and often either pregnant or still suckling a child, she may work 10 to 14 hours a day at the anvil in addition to grinding grain to make bread, carrying water, cooking, and looking after the children.

But until her sons grow strong enough to share her job, she must swing the hammer to help her husband earn a meager living. During a few months in early spring and fall, they may work from dawn into night beating iron bars into plowshares, sickles, hoes, wheel rims, and bullock shoes for busy farmers. On such a day, they can net as much as 10 rupees, less than $1.50, or about 15 cents a plowshare. Among the

White-hot iron in a charcoal fire awaits the light hammer of an aged Lohar camping on the outskirts of Delhi. His wife works a bellows, pumping air under the coals to heat the iron to about 3,800° F. For small items the man works alone. But beating out plowshares or shovels requires a ten-pound sledgehammer and a helper, usually his wife. She stands before the anvil and swings the sledge in rhythmic crashes upon the softened iron.

SATYA PAL RUHELA, *ranking authority on the Gaduliya Lohars, teaches the sociology of education at the Jamia Millia Islamia in New Delhi.*

Smoking the hookah begins the day for
Chelaji, sitting with his wife Choti and
daughter-in-law Pooni, who mixes
cornbread in front of his son Harji's
house at Mangliawas. Harji and his
brother Gopi (holding baby) built
houses on a camping site given them
by the village. One of the few Gaduliya
Lohar families settled year round, they
still live outside, prizing the house as a
status symbol and storing equipment
and grain indoors. At Bikholie, partly
settled Lohar women thresh bajra,
or millet. Between work-circuits, and
during the summer monsoon, their families park by their mud huts. But most
Lohar women, like the one at right, run
a household by the side of the road
within the space under, just beside, and
inside the family bullock cart.

Centuries of sunset have cast their glow on the wall of Chitorgarh
(below). Dawn gleams on island and lakeside palaces within. From this
Rajput citadel, legend says, the Lohars in 1568 escaped by a remote gate
(below, right) when the Moslem emperor Akbar took the fort. Destitute,

Lohars, a lazy person is considered as immoral as one who steals, and only a little less sinful than one who kills a sacred cow or cobra.

A visitor should never interrupt or disturb a blacksmith at work. So on this very warm October day when I arrived at Harji and Gopi's place, I sat down on the fiber cording of a wooden cot to watch Harji and his wife Pooni from the shade of Gopi's cart. Such heavy, open carts — *gaduliyas* — with pointed front, two large wooden wheels, and metal-covered body, have lumbered behind pairs of bullocks along Rajasthan's roads for 400 years or more. About 4,000 Gaduliya Lohar families, or some 25,000 persons, now live inside, underneath, and alongside the carts. In groups of 3 to 15 carts they travel five or six miles a day and then park in a line by the road outside villages and towns. Word spreads — "The Lohars have come!" — and customers bring tools to be mended, or orders for sickles and plowshares.

Here at his house, Harji was squatting on the ground behind his anvil and keeping his full attention on the glowing metal. Tongs in his left hand, he turned and shifted the iron bar between strokes of Pooni's sledgehammer. Between her regularly timed and carefully aimed blows, Harji struck the hot metal with a small hammer, refining the shape of the plowshare they were making.

Taller than his wife, Harji is slight in build, has medium-brown skin, and even, delicate features. Like most Lohar men, except for the very old, he wears no beard but has a full mustache. It increases his self-confidence, he once told me, especially during quarrels when he twists it at his opponent.

I was surprised to see his hair close-clipped in a popular Rajasthani style. Always before he had worn it in the old Lohar way — a four-inch strip shaved from forehead to crown, leaving long thick bunches of hair to hang over ears and back of the neck. I have heard from Harji and others that this style was designed by their ancestors when they first lost their high Rajput caste, became nomads, and used disguises to protect themselves from the conquering Moslem armies.

Harji, a highly articulate if illiterate man about 40 years old, has on several occasions told me of the events that caused the Lohars' fall from Rajput warrior dignity to poor wanderers so low in social status that their women are not permitted to draw water from the village wells. They must stand and wait until a higher-caste person comes to draw water and consents to fill the Lohar jar.

The story tells how the Lohars, or ironworkers, had served for a long time as weapon-makers at the Rajput fort of Chitorgarh in southern Rajasthan. In February 1568, just the night before the Mogul emperor Akbar and his army finally took the fort, the Rajput Lohars escaped by an unguarded gate and a secret path. Sickened by the slaughter at the fort, scorned as cowards, and grieved at their loss of livelihood, the destitute Lohars expressed their feelings in five vows: They would not live settled in houses, nor use a light to see in darkness, nor keep a rope to draw water from wells, nor carry their cots in standing position but only with legs pointing skyward, nor return to Chitorgarh Fort until it was free.

degraded below the Rajput caste, the Lohars took vows for a nomadic life of menial labor.

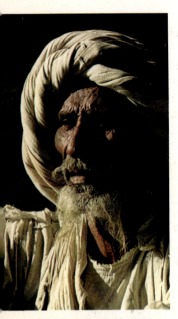

Work-scarred Chelaji has seen years of poverty. At age 10, his grandson Bhoma not only attends school but also teaches "his dearest friend"—the pet parrot his family can now afford.

I think the story of their origin as nomads can be considered more truth than myth. They still hate Moslems, the one group they say they will never work for. They still speak of themselves as fallen Rajputs. Their funeral-pyre incantation refers to Chitorgarh, and in rural southern Rajasthan, where their way of life has changed least, they still observe all the vows taken after the fall of the fort.

Since leaving Chitorgarh, they have lived in small family groups, each moving from village to village along its own prescribed circuit of about 50 miles. They wander in Rajasthan and the adjoining states. Only during the three hottest, wet summer months do they stop. Then they park in groups—I have seen as many as 200 carts in one camp— to wait out the rains and heat of the monsoon. Wherever they park, they work strenuously at their anvils, just as Harji and Pooni were doing the day I came to ask for help.

I became aware that the heavy thudding of the hammer had stopped. I saw Harji thrust the half-finished plowshare into the fiery coals filling a shallow hole in the ground beside him. Sparks and flames crackled and rose as Harji's 13-year-old daughter Ganga and her two younger brothers took turns working the bellows. Harji could now safely look up to see who had come. With a big smile, he scrambled to his feet. "*Maad Sab! Ram, Ram!* Teacher, Sir! Blessed be the name of the God Ram! Look, everybody—our friend the teacher has come!" He put his work-blackened palms together and raised his hands in front of his face, just as I was doing in the usual Indian greeting.

He was dressed in a *bakhtari*, a long-sleeved, rather tight shirt, and a *dhoti*, a five-yard length of white cloth ingeniously draped and tied into calf-length trousers. Both were soiled from many days' sweat and soot and dirt. His wife Pooni pulled her odhani over her long braid of black, oiled hair, and greeted me with just a broad smile. She called to Harji's mother, Choti, lying on a cot in front of Gopi's house nearby. As Choti rose and shuffled toward me, I asked, "How is the old man, Harji's father—Chelaji?" She gave the reply I had learned to expect: "He's lying there on his cot, not feeling well, for today he has no money for his opium."

I sat down with Harji and told him my problem. "Yes, I know Nathu," he said. "My oldest son Todu is betrothed to a distant cousin of Nathu's. I saw Nathu's brother-in-law just yesterday at the Lamana cattle fair, and that probably means Nathu's cart isn't too far away. So we'll go to the fair and find out exactly which village of the twenty or so in his circuit you'll find him at. The fair is just a little walk down the road, maybe ten minutes."

Gopi, he added, had gone to the fair with Todu and Harji's 16-year-old married son Halu. Halu's wife, also 16, had not come yet to live with him although the wedding took place five years ago. She would not join him until she had strength enough to swing the great hammer—perhaps after a few months more. Todu, now 18, had been betrothed when he was 10 to a baby; he would marry her next year and, unlucky man, wait several tedious years for her to live with him.

"As soon as I finish this plowshare, we'll go," Harji told me. "It's just as well that I go and find out what Gopi's doing. He went to trade a bullock, but you know he's the gossipy kind and might stay all night telling funny stories and drinking wine."

Of course Harji's ten-minute walk turned into an hour-long hike. I had plenty of time to ask him about Nathu's songs. "These days he sings mostly religious songs he makes himself," Harji said. "A few years back he liked to sing a lot of verses he made up about government Lohar settlements. They were all complaints, and everybody got tired of them after a while. Nathu heard these complaints from his cousin Koora, who once lived in the Lohar colony at Khanpura. They had enough complaints for a hundred verses."

In April 1955 Koora had heard our late Prime Minister Nehru say that Lohars and other nomads in India—14 groups in Rajasthan alone—ought to stop wandering. The government had chosen the Gaduliya Lohars as the first group in Rajasthan to receive land and money for a settlement. Mr. Nehru spoke during a state-organized convention that brought Lohars to the great fortress city of Chitorgarh for the first time in four centuries. Harji was there as leader for his band, and for a large section of the 4,000 Lohar men who had dared to come.

"I saw Lohar women all along the road to Chitorgarh and at the railroad stations crying and wailing that day, praying to Ram Deo, Kali, Khetla—all the Hindu and Gaduliya Lohar gods," Harji once told me. "They believed that the men who went to Chitorgarh would never return. The goddess of the fort, Kali, would kill them, they thought, for breaking the vow not to return there."

But nothing happened to the men. Eventually a few were persuaded to try living a settled life. Koora went to the colony at Khanpura, four miles outside Ajmer and just across the road from the odoriferous city dump. He never completed the house he tried clumsily to build for himself; it cost more than his life savings, the sale price of his wife's gold nose ring and silver anklets, and the government loan—amounting to $100—which his family is still struggling to pay back. A well for drinking water was finally started but not finished. Land fit to farm never materialized and Koora didn't know how to farm anyway. The colony's blacksmith shop floundered and failed. Koora shortly took to his cart again, as did almost all the other 350 Lohar families in a dozen other colonies with similar stories. Many had feared that their goddess Aie Lacha would curse them if they settled down; no doubt they took to the road again with relief. At least they could earn enough rupees as traveling blacksmiths to feed themselves.

They could gain a bit more by buying and selling bullocks the farmers need to pull plows and heavy wagons or to thresh grain. Often Lohar men make small deals in cattle. But their big chances come with the numerous cattle fairs held in Rajasthan east of sacred Pushkar Lake, from late August until the mammoth fair and religious festival at Pushkar itself in early November.

From the tree-lined highway, Harji and I could see the Lamana fair tent-shops, the moving mass of white bullocks and black water buffaloes, spread out over a flat expanse of campgrounds. An occasional lacy *babul* tree or white-trunked *pipal* offered a few spots of shade.

We squeezed through the turbaned crowd of men. We walked past the two rows of tents where men were squatting to cook over glowing charcoal for their customers. They fried wheat pancakes—*puris*—in deep fat until they puffed out like popovers. On the inside wall of a large pottery jug broken in half, they baked thin bread cakes, *chapattis*, another favorite food in Rajasthan and other states.

We stepped through a row of cobblers sitting on the ground under their big black umbrellas, and went behind the tent of the honorary magistrate of the fair who settles price arguments. Under a skimpy *khejra*, or acacia, tree, just by several *tongas*—small, lightweight carts attached like trailers to the Lohar cart—stood a circle of two dozen men. They were hovering around a white bullock. His red-painted horns made him appear to have won a prize, and little bells tinkled around his neck enticingly.

"Look—that's Gopi holding the bullock and I think he's closing the deal," Harji said. We joined the crowd to listen. Red-turbaned Gopi, small, light-skinned, his black eyes glinting with bright humor, was speaking with exaggerated dismay to a white-turbaned farmer.

"I swear by your neck that I am selling him at a loss and you offer me 50 rupees below my price! Oh no, I can't do that," Gopi said. His customer began turning away, muttering, "What loss? You've actually raised your price since this morning."

Immediately Gopi's expression changed to one of appeal, and he reached out to pat his escaping customer's chin affectionately. "This bullock is gold. *Sono che, sono*—it is gold, yes gold. I am giving it quite cheap. He is as strong as an elephant. You can have him for 350 rupees." The farmer hesitated, then shook his head. "No, no, it's too much, I can't pay so much. Besides, he's thin and starved."

They haggled on. Gopi repeated the Rajasthani words *"Soro dido chun*—I am giving it cheap" like the refrain to a temple chant. They finally agreed at 325 rupees and the farmer led the red-horned beast away, still hearing Gopi insist, "Soro dido chun!"

The little crowd broke up laughing and talking. Gopi kept his face businesslike, not revealing whether he had made a profit or loss.

"That is right, Teacher," he said to me after a round of greetings. "This fair does not rank among the best of my life, yet it has stayed above the worst. As you know, *nafo nuksan apani takderan ro howe*— profit and loss depend upon one's fate."

Gopi told us where Kooka, son of Nathu's uncle Gheesya, could be found. We picked our way through the cattle, people, campfires, carts, animal droppings, food tents, and bunches of fodder to a large *neem* tree. But Kooka had left just minutes before to catch the bus home. Harji, Gopi, and I ran for the highway, and found Kooka waiting under a wide-spreading banyan tree.

Harji quickly introduced us and explained my wish to record Nathu's songs. At once Kooka invited us to spend the night at Nathu's camp. "Nathu will be happy to know you are a friend of Harji and Gopi. He'll play his harmonium and sing as long as you like." In a few

"Mama!" wails a Lohar baby at the doorway of his mud-and-cow-dung hut. Lohar families, permitted to build houses at Bikholie village, have made the settlement a seasonal base. A government program to settle Lohars as farmers failed after about 350 families had built huts in a dozen colonies. Discouraged by poor land, lack of farming skill and even of water, they soon returned to the road and the traveling anvil.

Easily draped odhani — *yards of cloth — lends grace to Lohar women. Tattoo of peacocks, a popular motif, may denote the desire to be beautiful or proclaim love for one's partner in life.*

Overleaf: Mingling with campfire smoke, grunts and reeking odors rise from the grounds at Pushkar Fair. Traders bring some 25,000 work animals, mostly valuable camels, to the great annual sale. At its fringes hundreds of Lohars who come specialize in bullock dealing, pleased to make a 10-percent profit — maybe 32 rupees, or about $4.

minutes we were standing inside the crowded bus, waving to Harji and watching Gopi walk toward a roadside wineshop.

When we stepped off the bus at the outskirts of Padla at twilight some 60 miles and three hours later, I saw four Gaduliya Lohar carts sitting beside the asphalt road. A sunshade of reed curtaining, the *sirki*, held up by corner posts and ridgepole, hung over each cart for privacy. Under the cart's pointed end and tongue sat short-legged wooden cots on which babies slept and small children lounged. Bullocks lay on the ground, chewing their cuds sleepily and flicking their tails at flies. Little boys climbed up on the axle brace and over the sideboards into the carts, dug around in the tangle of ragged bedding, clothes bags, sacks of grain, tools, and pieces of scrap iron, then climbed down again to bring an implement to a parent. Seated on the ground, women patted out *roti* cakes of wet cornmeal between their palms and baked them in a cooking bowl over a heap of coals.

I saw a very dark, lanky, bearded man with a wide white turban and a sprawling gray mustache, squatting behind an anvil. He grunted loudly each time his teen-age son brought down the great hammer: Thud! "Ugh!" Thud! "Ugh!" Thud! With no grunt as signal to continue, the hammer-swinger stopped, and his father shoved the half-finished sickle back into the bed of hot coals. Immediately he stood up, gave me a greeting, and spoke hurriedly to Kooka. "What did the *panchayat* at the fair decide about Baldeva's breaking off his daughter's betrothal and giving her to another for a bigger bride-price?" His curiosity was natural — Baldeva's offense was grave.

Before replying to his question, Kooka introduced me to him: Gheesya, the leader of this small sub-band, his father and Nathu's uncle. Kooka also told him why I had come. But Gheesya had far more interest in what happened at the panchayat meeting, from which he had begged off. The panchayat is India's ancient council of acknowledged leaders within a village or caste or, among the Lohars, a band. Often Lohars hold their meetings during cattle fairs where leaders will gather for trade; they settle disputes and punish misbehavior.

Gheesya repeated his question and Kooka answered, "They haven't decided yet. They're just sitting in a circle on the fairgrounds, for hours and hours, passing the hookah around, whispering to each other once in a while, but not deciding anything. Maybe tomorrow."

I could well understand Gheesya's sigh. I once sat all one day and evening waiting for a band panchayat to tell me whether it would ask its people to cooperate in my study of Gaduliya Lohar life.

Each sub-band elects one or more *panchas*, usually for their ability to smooth ruffled feelings within the small group, and for their good sense when they sit in council. The band council judges more serious matters, such as bride-price, bad debts, the wearing of novel clothing, marital quarrels, elopements — Lohars disapprove love matches. I haven't heard of a case of stealing within the group, for the Lohars strongly believe that their goddess Kali of Chitorgarh will blind a thief.

On rare occasions a regional council of panchas will make a major decision. About 200 years ago, it is said, a great council decided to

Proper male attire in-cludes headgear — a non-expert winds ten yards of lightly starched cloth into place. Most Lohars wear red turbans while the father lives, change to white when he dies.

allow widows to remarry, thus breaking an upper-caste tradition that Lohars had always observed.

Sometimes a band panchayat cannot settle a quarrel. Then it sends for the supreme *panch* of the region. Southern Rajasthan bands call on an exemplary man, Kalu, who inherited this status from his father; his word is law. Punishments range from giving a great feast for two or three hundred people to throwing down corn for wild pigeons.

Having told Gheesya all the news from Lamana Fair, Kooka guided me to a cart just across the road. There a woman sat on the ground, swaying back and forth gently as she pushed a flat, heavy stone around and around on top of another to grind corn. Nathu, her husband, she told us shyly, had not returned from town where he'd gone to sell sickles and knives and to buy vegetables and sweets.

Nathu arrived after dark, carrying his purchases and exuding good spirits. He had sold all his implements for a few pennies each, and celebrated with smoking opium-tinged tobacco in the hookah and gossiping for an hour or two. Enthusiastically he welcomed me, my battery-operated tape recorder, and my request for his songs.

"But first let us sit on my cot and eat a little roti with some fine hot chilis and chutney and some *gwarphali* [wild pea pods] my wife has cooked. Then I will call my kinsman Ollo to clack the cymbals against the long tongs, and you, Kooka, to strike the finger cymbals. I can play on the harmonium songs praising Ganesh, elephant-headed son of the god Shiva, and songs praising Ram Deo.

"You will love the song about our god Ram Deo on his horse riding about to cure the woes of poor people, sick people, barren women, people afraid of ghosts and demons that blind and kill. . . ."

He sang long into the night. Grown-ups and children from all the carts gathered to sit on the ground around us, sometimes clapping or grunting in rhythm to the bell-like cymbals and Nathu's catchy if monotonous tunes repeated for dozens of verses. At first the coals of the cooking fire gave off a dim light. I could watch the expressive face of Nathu underneath his wide white turban, and his long brown fingers on the keys of his harmonium. Then it became so dark — the Lohar vow not to use a light was observed — that I operated my tape recorder and Nathu played by touch.

Nathu saved his most impressive song until last. He had composed it himself, describing at length the flight of a dead man's soul. Higher and higher into heaven it goes, where it finds the key to salvation — understanding of everything and right knowledge — and where all base desires and emotions vanish.

O Soul, you're now married to the Dweller of the sky!
O Soul, you're now destined to ascend to the sky to join
    your Bridegroom!
O Soul, there's neither shadow nor sun in His wonderful land!
O Soul, I too wish to reach that land where only rare saints can go!

Nathu wanted to tell his wife and small child to give up their place high in the cart, safe from snakes and wandering animals, and let me sleep there. But I begged off, for I am taller than the space is long, and the grain bags and scattered tools make a lumpy mattress. Once some years ago I tried it. My head rested on the cover of the enclosed front of the cart, called the *thalia,* a sort of cupboard where valuables like nose and ear rings, cosmetics, spices, butter, and money are kept. The sleeper must not lie with his feet on the thalia lest he insult the statue of the goddess Kali inside. Nor should he prop his feet on the rear board, for that's the shelf for small clay jars containing cooked food. I hardly slept at all on that occasion and climbed out of the cart at day-break, aching and stiff.

So now I begged Nathu to let me sleep outside on a cot. It took a long time, it seemed to me, for everyone to settle down. Lohars like to talk and for hours Nathu's relatives spoke back and forth between their carts in sharp loud voices.

I was suddenly awakened just before dawn by a commotion—groans, calls, excited talk. My first thought was of an incident a few years ago in the Chitorgarh district when a tiger crept up to a Lohar cot one night and dragged away a sleeping child.

But the Lohars here were not losing a child, they were about to gain one. Gheesya's daughter-in-law Kukkoo had started having labor pains. Everybody had run over to look at her. Faint light began to dilute the heavy darkness, and her mother-in-law Pyari dragged the sirki from the cart and sat it upright on the ground to screen Kukkoo's cot. Pyari qualified as midwife because she had borne several children and watched the birth of others. One of her tasks was to shoo away a flock of staring children and scold them each time they crept back. She and the other women from the four carts took turns consoling Kukkoo, rubbing her abdomen, and wiping her face.

At Gheesya's cart, I joined the men, including Kukkoo's silent and wide-eyed husband, Bhairon. "Tell us, Uncle, what will you feed us to celebrate the birth of your grandson?" joked Nathu.

"Make sure it's a grand *son,*" proclaimed Gheesya, "and you can take your pick—goat meat, sweetened rice, sweets, wine, opium—anything you want!" They joked and laughed louder and louder as the noises behind the sirki increased. All at once I saw in the widening dawn light that Pyari was climbing on the wheel of a cart and pawing fran-tically among the dusty bedclothes and grain sacks.

"What are you looking for?" called her husband. "A sickle! A sickle! To cut the baby's cord!" she cried. "You make so many sickles and today nobody has a one!" Bhairon reached in his father's cart and pulled out a sickle. "Here—I made it yesterday—it's good and sharp," he said, holding it out to Pyari. She grabbed it and ran.

"It's a girl," said Gheesya flatly. "If it had been a boy, we'd have heard about it." He sighed deeply. Everyone was very quiet.

In silence we ate our breakfast of cold roti and chutney. The men got out their hammers and tongs, bars of iron, and pieces of scrap metal that the children had collected the day before. Gheesya started the fire and then squatted to touch the anvil as he whispered his morning prayer: "O Anvil, give us a full belly and keep the quarrelsome cus-tomers away from us today." (Continued on page 49)

Sanctified by the creator god Brahma, waters of Pushkar Lake purify the souls of more than 100,000 November fair-goers, including hundreds of Lohars, and assure them a place in heaven. Women and men line up along different portions of the lake to bathe at the foot of temple steps.

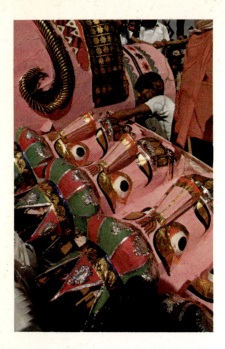

Firecrackers explode around a giant
effigy, and nine-headed monster Ravana
(right and detail above) dies, slain by
the hero-god Ram. This climax to the
ten-day Dussehra festival of outdoor
dramas draws some Lohars to the
displays in Jaipur (right). For Divali,
festival of lights, Lohars at Udaipur
set oil lamps ablaze: Lakshmi, goddess
of prosperity, will ignore an unlit home.

Silver-white sword hilt of wedding regalia indicates the bridegroom's presence among kinsmen as Deva, 16, arrives in a bullock cart (below) at his bride's camp outside Kapasan. The solemn groom (right), engaged since childhood and kept from seeing his betrothed, will not look at the face of his bride, Kakku, until the second day of ceremonies. Then they get acquainted during games, such as competing to find a ring in a pan of cloudy water (left); in one game he removes her veil. Two more days of ritual, feasts, and teasing jokes await them at his camp. Usually the bride then rejoins her family to grow to womanhood. But Kakku, 16, stayed with Deva to live in his family's cart-home.

At Pushkar Fair, bullocks and a gypsy-tongued Lohar trader wait for customers. The smithy brings about $10 a month to the Lohar below. He worships his anvil as the dwelling of the goddess of wealth, but the crude pieces he makes on it compete poorly with those made by machines.

His 12-year-old daughter Bhanwari began lifting and pressing the goatskin bellows, and another day of work began. Tomorrow early they would pile cots and pots, anvil and newborn baby, and all the members of the family into the cart for another ride on groaning wooden wheels to the next village.

I saw this family some weeks later at Kapasan when I went there with Harji for the wedding of his cousin Deva to Gheesya's niece Kakku. Gheesya's cart carried three nested cots, legs to the sky, and six people. They arrived at the bride's camp just as the groom's procession of two carts approached. The 16-year-old groom looked rather sullen, for he and his relatives had waited three hours at the train station before the bride's family sent carts to fetch them.

Gheesya had brought many presents—turbans, kanchalis, odhanis. Lohars invariably spend more for weddings than they can afford. Often a father will take out loans from town merchants, at stiff interest, to pay for bride bangles, ear and toe ornaments, gifts for the couple and their female relatives, food and wine and opium for hundreds of guests.

Harji and I ate roti and chutney with the bride's family, but the groom's party would go unfed for hours, until the end of the first important ceremony, the *toran marana.*

By brilliant kerosene lamps—permissible because they were rented, not owned by Lohars—we watched the rites with a noisy, slightly drunken crowd of about 200 people. The bridegroom, dressed in pink with silver ornaments and a sword, faced his mother-in-law and her singing women companions. She moved a plate with four burning candles, a small pot of water, and pieces of bread and molasses around the groom's head, while his relatives began to sing:
O mother-in-law behold your son-in-law's appearance,
Lest you should complain afterward!
Now the crowd moved to the sacred fire—prepared by a Brahmin—where the bride waited. The groom, who since his betrothal ten years before had never seen his marriage partner, got no glimpse of her now behind her bridal veil. He could only sit beside her, hold her hand briefly during the hand-clasping ceremony, and look at her from the corner of his eye during the Brahmin's exhortation. It was about marriage, and in ancient Sanskrit, which no one could understand. At last the bride's odhani was knotted to the groom's *chehda,* or sash, and they began to walk the seven nuptial rounds about the sacred fire. The tipsy groom never quite made seven times, but the bride did and was then entitled to sit at her husband's right, a married girl.

The ceremonies ended with the bride being adopted by her husband's father, and throwing on the crowd handfuls of grain from his cart—a symbol of hoped-for prosperity. "I have completed my task," said the groom's father as he put his hands on the children's heads to bless them: "Remain alive for ages, live well, work well, eat well."

At last the groom's party could rush to the open kitchen area. There waited a great cauldron of *dal,* or split gram-pea soup, big baskets full of puris, plates of *halwa*—wheat flour roasted in boiled butter and sweetened—and bowls heaped high with boiled and spiced potatoes.

Everyone must have felt exhausted. Both families had sat up all the previous night, singing prayers for prosperity and happiness, the climax to a week of nightly feasting, dancing, and singing. But long after Harji and I stretched out on borrowed cots, I heard lively joking, laughing, and raucous singing. I hoped that the bride and groom, in their separate camps, were resting for the next day's events—ceremonies to appease malicious Khetla, illegitimate son of goddess Aie Lacha; a ceremony for the groom to knock down with his sword three wooden birds fastened to an improvised doorframe representing *toran*, the Hindu marriage booth; games allowing the groom to see his wife for the first time; a boisterous evening feast ending with the burning of coconut meat to ensure fertility. But they probably stayed up all night too.

Harji and I left on the third morning as the panchayat witnessed the payment of the second half of the bride-price, which normally totals about $12, and the handing over of the bride's dowry: head pads for cushioning water jugs, bangles, comb, and wooden fan for herself; a kanchali for each of a half-dozen in-laws.

Usually the bride and groom are small children and they must wait many years before the simple *muklawa* or post-wedding ceremony is performed and the girl comes to live with her husband. But Kakku was 16 and already strong enough to swing the hammer. She went with Deva back to his cart, shared with parents and three brothers. For a year or so she would obey an often scolding, resentful mother-in-law, swing the hammer for her husband, and endure his brothers' teasing.

But finally the day would come when Deva's father would give them their own cart and bullocks and tools, the son's inheritance. "That's the really expensive part of marrying off a son," Harji remarked to me on the bus back to Mangliawas. "By the time a man has paid for a cart for each of several boys, he's as poor as the day he started. Poorer, maybe. In old age he must depend on his youngest son."

The bus passed a line of Gaduliya Lohar carts parked by the highway. I saw a baby boy, naked and barely able to stand, all by himself at an anvil, hitting a piece of metal with a rock. "He already knows what he'll be when he grows up," I said to Harji.

Harji looked thoughtful. After a while, he said: "I will have it easier, and my boys will have it easier now that I have settled by my house in a good village. Especially my son Dalu who goes to school and is number one in his class of 50 boys. I think that if a person is educated it is good for him these days. Gopi and I have no education and we have to sit before our fire and anvil from early morning to night every day. Our blood turns to water and our eyes become red hot. I have seen that educated people have a comfortable life. If any of us Lohars can have such a life, it will bring peace to our soul. But how can we find this education? I think it will come from God and man cooperating. If our caste is to be uplifted, man must do something, and God must also do something.

"If He doesn't, then, as we are today, so we will remain. . . ."

Slowly, slowly, bullocks pull groaning Lohar carts past Kishangarh. In
early morning, they start for a village a few miles away. There the
nomads build their fire, set the anvil, and hope for trade. For most Lohars,
their goddess Aie Lacha's curse weighs heavy: "May you always
wander in hunger. May you never eat to your heart's content."

Autumn day dawns in the Rab' al Khālī — the Empty Quarter — as an Āl Murrah family of 15 members breaks camp

Custom Rules "the Pure Ones,"
ĀL MURRAH Bedouin of Arabia's

By Donald P. Cole, *Ph.D.*
Illustrations by Tor Eigeland

THOMAS J. ABERCROMBIE, N.G.S. STAFF

Only a few hardy Bedouin, skilled in desert ways, penetrate the desolation of Arabia's sandy wastes.

Empty Sands

Obedient to custom, men of the Āl 'Azab clan eat in silence, dipping right hands only into a dish of rice and camel meat. The author, seated before the end of the tent wall, joins them in camp near summer grazing.

54

ONE MORNING in late autumn I stopped my camel and turned to look in all directions. I saw nothing but flat, barren land with only the faint white line of a sand dune, maybe 20 miles away, to break its monotony. No rain had fallen for several years and only a few clumps of withered grass remained to suggest the possibility of life.

Marzūq, a Bedouin youth of about 18 years, had told me to look for five she-camels strayed from a herd of seventy or so. He had said that I would find them in the direction where the sun sets in winter, just over the horizon. He wanted me to track them and bring them back.

Exhilarated and a bit afraid, I was alone deep in the Rab' al Khālī, or Empty Quarter, some 200,000 square miles of desert in southern Arabia. This land boasts no permanent settlements; its wells are scattered and I could never hope to find them by myself. I could not count on meeting oil workers or geological survey teams.

"These are the Sands, what others call the Quarter of Emptiness," Marzūq had told me. "Only the sināfīyīn, the really skilled and daring Bedouin, ever come here."

I jogged on, however, and soon forgot my fear. I knew Marzūq would never abandon me. We were companions, "brothers," he had said in Arabic, and these Āl Murrah Bedouin, accustomed to the rigors of life in the Empty Quarter, value loyalty to personal companions even to the point of death. I also knew that Marzūq, or any boy of his tribe, "the House of Murrah," could easily follow the tracks of my camel across gravel plains or among the prints of other camels. If I did not return by late afternoon, he would come to look for me.

After about an hour, I spotted the five black she-camels and soon had them moving. About midday I saw Marzūq's herd and rode to it silently in the stillness of noon before the hot afternoon winds began to blow. In summer this land is an inferno, with temperatures reaching as high as 130° F. or more, but now it was a pleasant 80. I found Marzūq himself lying on the bare plain. He had pulled his red-and-white checkered headdress over his face and used his rifle butt, padded with the skins of gazelle heads, as a pillow.

Gently I tapped my camel's neck to make her kneel. I dismounted, found a shrub that would shade my head and shoulders, and lay down. Resting there, I thought of the old Bedouin who said that when he lay down beside his camels at midday and the breeze cooled his tired, sweating body, he would not trade places with any king.

I felt my own satisfaction over my first effort at camel herding. I wanted to please Marzūq and show him that, although I came from the cities of America, I could learn from him. Younger than I and completely illiterate, he had a specialist's knowledge of his desolate homeland. He had taught me much about the ways his people eke out a living during the two months since his elder brother, Al Kurbī, had brought me into the Rab' al Khālī in his old pickup truck.

On arriving in Saudi Arabia, I hoped to perfect my command of

After two years with the Āl Murrah and one of study in California, DONALD P. COLE *now teaches anthropology at the American University in Cairo.*

Kneeling baggage camel (right) patiently waits as women prepare to lift a sayyārah, or riding litter, to his back. After breaking camp, women and children trail the caravan (top) on a short trek to the next well; on longer marches they usually ride in the litters. Women manage many details of camp life, including loading and moving, while men herd the milk camels. Two of the author's companions tend their camels: Marzūq (above left) watches a grazing herd while Ḥurrān milks a fine Sharfā.

THOMAS J. ABERCROMBIE, NATIONAL GEOGRAPHIC STAFF (ABOVE AND BELOW)

THOMAS J. ABERCROMBIE, N.G.S. STAFF (BELOW)

Frolicsome Āl Murrah boys dash across desert sands near a salty well. For sport, youngsters race and wrestle; at about age 10, however, they start herding camels and learning the ways of men. Tribesmen (left) hoist water-filled truck inner tubes—obtained from oil crews—to the back of a pack camel. Inner tubes, one of the few Āl Murrah accommodations to the modern world, replace smaller, leaky goatskin water bags.

spoken Arabic and begin field research for a dissertation in social anthropology. I hardly dreamed of studying such an isolated group as the Āl Murrah; but when various princes and government officials expressed interest in data on this tribe, I jumped at the chance.

The officials wanted to make precise and scientific plans for the King Faisal Settlement Project at Ḥaraḍ. Here the government has spent more than 20 million dollars to provide wells and irrigation on some 8,000 acres of land for agricultural use by the Āl Murrah and other tribes. I was glad to think my research could aid them. Moreover, no professional anthropologist had ever studied an Arab tribe so little changed, the most widespread in the area.

By chance I met Rāshid ibn Ṭālib ibn Shuraim, heir of the tribe's paramount chief. His father, Emir Ṭālib, had come with a retinue of elders to Ar Riyāḍ, the capital, to discuss tribal affairs with King Faisal, and Rāshid invited me to an evening feast in the desert just outside the city. He reminded me to kiss his father's nose when I met him, as a greeting of deference; and explained to him my wish to share the life of the Bedouin. The old man welcomed me and invited me to sit next to him. He discreetly observed everything I did—how I drank the tiny cups of coffee, savored the incense when it was passed around, how I answered questions.

After a while he said: "You and Rāshid are brothers. You both study and speak English, which I don't know. It is good to study in schools and I want Rāshid to travel and to know all the world. But it is also good to know the knowledge of the desert. There they have the purest camels, many gazelles, clean sand, and fresh air. There you will learn everything. Welcome, O my son."

If Emir Ṭālib prefers his black tents to an air-conditioned city home, he acts in accordance with the feelings of most of his tribe. Known as "the wolves of the desert" to other Saudi Arabians, the Āl Murrah scorn cities, which they consider corrupt or polluted. Their love for their camels and for the freshness of their environment makes them reluctant to settle down as farmers at Ḥaraḍ.

Ranging over an area as large as France, the 15,000 Āl Murrah inhabit the central and eastern two-thirds of the Rab' al Khālī. They divide themselves into subtribes, each with clans, lineages, and extended families. All claim pure descent from Qaḥṭān, legendary ancestor of the southern Arabs. In a land where genealogy largely defines social identity, they rank as ʿarab al ʿarbā, Arabs of the Arabs.

My friend Marzūq comes from the Āl ʿAzab clan of the powerful Āl Fuhaidah subtribe. His grandfather and kinsmen carried out some of the most successful and daring camel-stealing raids in the annals of eastern and southern Arabia. Consequently, he said, his clan's milk and riding camels—all marked with a single *wasm*, or brand—make up the finest herds in the peninsula.

The Āl ʿAzab also stand out as one of the most far-ranging of all the Āl Murrah, indeed of all Bedouin. Moving always in search of the best grasses, they sometimes spend a winter and spring in the extreme northeast of Saudi Arabia or southern Iraq, and then cross the Empty

Quarter to spend the next winter grazing the pastures near Najrān far to the southwest, after traveling 1,200 miles. Other Āl Murrah, in the habit of shorter migrations, call them "nomads of the nomads."

As we rode along behind our herd after the midday rest, I asked Marzūq which other clans frequent the Empty Quarter. He named three or four. "All the Āl Murrah," he explained, "might send some camels to graze here during some seasons, especially during long droughts in the north. Only those of us who own wells here come every year. Some of the other clans have sold their camels and have only sheep and goats, so they stay near the towns in the north. Besides, their sons study in the schools now and they would get lost here."

He glanced at the sun and said, "Time to pray." Immediately we turned our camels, made them kneel, and dismounted. While the herd drifted on, he drew a semicircle in the sand to indicate the direction of Mecca and then intoned the ancient Moslem call to prayer, affirming that "There is no God but God." For lack of water, he knelt and rubbed sand over his hands and face in the ritual ablutions of Islam. Then, purified, he faced westward toward the holy Ka'aba in Mecca, and we recited silently the first chapter of the Koran and other short prayers.

We remounted and he shouted, "I'll race you!" In a flash we were off, brandishing our camel-sticks just by the ears of our camels to make a whirring sound and shouting "hinnnnh!" to urge them on. After a hundred yards we caught up with the herd and Marzūq laughingly claimed that he had won—although we had stayed neck and neck. I challenged him to produce witnesses, and he shouted, "I and my camel!" Both of us rode young Omani thoroughbreds and it had been just about all I could manage to stay on.

At a chain of sand dunes about 60 feet high, running east-west, our camels wound their way up the slope single file. They bounded down the other side, kicking up their heels and bucking and rushing head-on toward some green bushes about six feet high. Marzūq called these 'abal and explained that they make the Empty Quarter habitable for folk who have camels. Rain once in four years suffices to keep them alive. "We can always find 'abal someplace, even when all the grasses and smaller bushes have died from lack of rain. Also, the camels love it, and it makes their milk really sweet."

He decided to let his camels feed here until nightfall. "You ride on ahead," he said. "You'll find Muḥammad and the others just to the south of that next dune."

Muḥammad, one of Marzūq's three older brothers, was standing on top of a dune, scanning the country with an old pair of binoculars. I dismounted, hobbled my camel, and began the polite greetings: "Peace be with you!"

"And with you peace!" he answered. "What is your condition?"

"May God protect you! How are you?"

"May God give you eyes! If God wills, you are not tired."

"The praise be to God!" I said.

"What is your news?" he asked, and I gave him a thumbnail sketch of what we had done. He grinned widely, took me by the hand in Arab

Tugging at a handmade camel's-hair rope, Āl 'Azab herders draw brackish

water from a 20-foot-deep well 62 miles southeast of Jabrin. Unfit for humans, the water satisfies stately milk camels (below) crowding at a leather
trough. For liquids, Āl Murrah rely mainly on camel's milk, coffee, and tea.

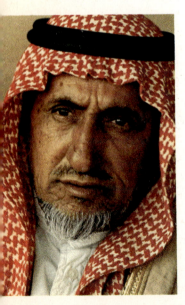

Gleaming with silver, an eight-inch curved dagger hangs at the waist of an Āl Murrah tribesman. Such heirloom blades mark the bearers as true Bedouin. Today, older men—contemporaries of Emir Ṭālib ibn Shuraim (below)—wear them as a sign of status.

fashion, and said, "Let's go get the coffee fire started." In the lee of the dune we reached the night's *manzil*—"place of alighting" or camp. We found only four big leather saddlebags filled with such things as rice, flour, dates, some clothing and a few cooking utensils, and two very large rubber inner tubes filled with water. Muḥammad explained that his elder brother Al Kurbī had taken their parents, his own wife, and all the children on ahead in his pickup. "We'll catch up with them tomorrow night or the next night, if God wills," he said.

Just then Muḥammad's young wife came up with a huge bundle of scrub firewood balanced on her head. She wished us peace and asked how we were. Then, letting the firewood drop to the ground, she straightened the black mask that revealed only her eyes and settled the black gauze that covered the top and back of her head. Rich clothing indicated her aristocratic birth: a long black dress with red embroidery along the borders, several strands of red beads, five or six silver bracelets on each arm, and a collection of 12 gold rings with jade, onyx, or turquoise settings. These she had tied on a string that she looped across the top of her head to hold the headdress in place.

Not all Bedouin women wear veils, but veiling and strict separation of the sexes characterize the most proper and religious Bedouin in Saudi Arabia. Muḥammad's wife—for me to name her would be shameful—did not tarry to chat, but demurely went over to the saddlebags for cooking utensils to prepare our main meal of the day.

Muḥammad and I made coffee and talked at leisure during the three hours that passed before we ate. Marzūq and another young man, Ibn Quray' of the Āl Jābir subtribe, joined us before sunset. Ibn Quray' had come hunting some stray camels and traveled as our guest. As such, he relied on his hosts for absolute protection. A guest in one's camp is a sacred trust; he must be defended even against one's closest kin.

At sunset we prayed, the fourth time that day. Only one more prayer, about two hours later, remained. Like most of the Bedouin of Saudi Arabia, the Āl Murrah follow the strict Hanbalite school of orthodox Sunni Islam and rigorously adhere to its rituals. Ibn Quray', who had already made the *Hajj*, or Pilgrimage to Mecca, led our prostrations in praise of God, the Compassionate, the Merciful, He that is most Great.

Muḥammad's wife prayed separately and silently behind a short tent wall that she had put up for privacy. There she removed her veil to approach her God with an open face. Only during prayers and within the bounds of Mecca during the Pilgrimage do such women take off their masklike veils. Customarily, I was told, they keep them on even when eating and when asleep at night.

After the final prayer Muḥammad called for supper, and his wife brought a huge plate of rice over which he poured melted *samn*, clarified butter. A hare he had shot early that morning graced the middle of the plate; he had skinned and cleaned it, and his wife had boiled it for a couple of hours in water with salt and onions for seasoning.

We four men gathered around the plate, kneeling on the left knee with the left hand behind the back. We waited for each to settle himself comfortably, murmured, "In the Name of God, the Compassionate, the Merciful," and began to eat. Each chose rice directly before him and gathered it up into a ball in the palm of the right hand to eat it. Muḥammad pulled meat from the hare and offered part of it to his guest, Ibn Quray', then some to me.

Such formality marks each meal as well as each greeting; and it would seem that in a life filled with rituals of politeness or prayer, these tribesmen feel little need for elaborate rites of passage — ceremonies for occasions of birth or marriage or death.

When we had supped, we stood up; Ibn Quray' prayed that his host's father and grandfathers might rest in Heaven, and we others asked God's blessing on all present. We rubbed our hands in sand to clean them and Muḥammad brought water to rinse them. Marzūq produced a bottle of cologne, and we splashed some on our hands and faces. Muḥammad took the tray of food back to his wife while the rest of us retired to the coffee fire, where Marzūq served sweetened mint tea.

We had eaten well tonight. The Bedouin do not consider meat an everyday need, although they will slaughter a sheep or a young camel in honor of any guest, rich or poor. Generous hospitality is a major obligation. But in the Rab' al Khālī, where guests are few, the Āl Murrah rarely eat meat except game. Gazelles make communal feasts for three or four households now and then; more often, hares hunted by fast saluki hounds supplement the rice.

From day to day, the Āl Murrah rely on camels for livelihood. The Bedouin love their camels, especially the young ones, and name each one. For some of their most prized camels they can recite the dams through 15 generations, and they never tire of talking or reciting poems about them. Camels give the tribes mobility; they supply hair for ropes and wool for clothing; above all, each female with an offspring gives as much as a gallon of milk daily for 11 months out of the year.

Late one afternoon I went out walking with a famous poet of the Āl Murrah, Al Ḥudayb. At least 80, he often berated the younger generations for their "easy living," not without justice. As usual, he skeptically questioned me about the customs of Americans: whether we marry our women or just take them in free liaison, whether we know how to sing like the Bedouin, whether we know about God and pray regularly, whether America has any nomads and whether they own camels. When I told him that we have few camels, he reasoned that we must be very poor, downtrodden people.

"You know, O my son," he said, "the first thing God created when He created the world was milk. And from this milk came all life, first mankind and then camels. Just as our own mothers gave us life with their milk when we were young and helpless, so the she-camels mother us all and keep us alive. The most precious of God's gifts to mankind and the world is milk. Those who follow the camels and live most exclusively off their sweet milk are the ones who live in greatest harmony with the Universe. Camelmen, my son, are the most blessed of all the world."

If camels sustain life and leisure, they also keep the Bedouin on the move. After a couple of months of short journeys — five or six miles a day—during the fall, news came to us of winter rains in the north, more than 500 miles away. Marzūq pointed out faint white clouds high in the northern sky and said he had seen lightning during the night. "*Inshallāh*, if God wills, we shall find rich grasses in the north and, if we have really good luck, we may find truffles as well! The rains are falling early this year."

In autumn the days were pleasant but at night the temperatures often dropped to near freezing. From mid-December until January we moved every day, from just after dawn until just before sunset, often covering 40 miles. As we traveled northward, more and more families joined us until all the Āl 'Azab clan's 35 tents and their respective herds came together. Each family tried to find the best route with the best grazing for its own camels, in a kind of jocular competition.

One day Al Kurbī and I climbed a small mountain near Jabrin, the major date-palm oasis of the Āl Murrah. I stood amazed. A great horde surged forward. At least 4,000 camels, steadily moving in long strides, dominated the landscape. Al Kurbī peered at them through his binoculars. In Bedouin understatement he murmured, "*Allāh karīm*, God is generous. The bounty is great."

The women, who deal with everything concerning the tents and household items, had loaded their powerful baggage camels with the goat's-hair tents, tapestries and rugs, sacks of rice and dates, pots and clothing. In small groups just behind the herds, they formed the only really colorful part of the great procession.

Women weave their own saddlebags in complex geometric patterns using brilliant hues of reds, oranges, and greens, interspliced by strips of white with special tribal designs in black. They had other bags of tanned leather with long red and white tassels. They themselves sat in magnificence in brightly colored *sayyārahs*—litters—rocked to and fro like small boats in troubled water as the huge camels walked slowly but continuously onward.

The youths and young men rode with their herds. Without fail, each sported a cartridge belt and carried his rifle, a truly prized possession. These Bedouin remember that no more than 40 years ago— before King 'Abd al-'Azīz ibn Sa'ud put a stop to it—the fierce "sport" of raiding made life in the desert a competition for survival.

Before sunset, the old men select campsites. Men hobble their camels, let them wander off to graze, make the coffee fires, and prepare to roast, grind, and serve the bitter coffee. Women arrive, guiding the baggage camels to the proper spot. For dismounting, they tap the great beasts lightly on the forelegs with camel-sticks and utter gargling sounds to make them kneel. They unload the camels and set up the tents, each with its brightly colored curtain to separate the men's section from the *ḥarīm* reserved for themselves and their children.

In the hour or so before the communal supper, men sip coffee at one tent or another, talking of camels and pastures. An old man tells a long story about a fight he and some cousins had as youths with foreign tribesmen in the south, across the Rab' al Khālī. Another tells how he and two others once tracked an ostrich a hundred miles before they

Like a Bedouin raider of past generations, Mas'ūd al Qaṭāmī straddles an Omani riding camel—bred for speed and comfort. He carries a rifle and dagger out of habit. Fierce warriors, the Āl Murrah took camels from neighboring tribes and developed superbly useful stock. Formal and detailed codes of chivalry governed Bedouin raiding, now illegal but a standard of valor just 40 years ago.

Wind-honed dunes curve beyond the goat's-hair tents of the Āl Fuhaidah subtribe near Az Zarnūqah, the Āl Murrah's northernmost sweet-water wells. Powerful winds drive sand along (left) as a blinding simoom sweeps the Empty Quarter. Camels (right) start to kneel before a gusty whirlwind veiling the tribe's major oasis of date palms at Jabrin.

caught up with it. Everybody crowds around the fire, engrossed in stories that all have heard many times before.

After supper the youths may gather to drink mint tea while a poet recites new poems, recently composed—among the Bedouin, poetry enjoys the highest honor. Toward midnight men offer large bowls of frothing fresh camel milk to their elders, then to one another. Marzūq insists that I drink, "to have power." Married men retire to the ḥarīms. We who are unmarried smooth out the sand in our section of the tent, wrap ourselves fully clothed in blankets, and lie down to sleep. Just before dawn the new day begins with the call to prayer.

So we passed 18 days and some 700 miles of travel—a fast journey as well as a long one—and reached a pasture area known as the Rubaydā'. Very good rains had fallen and we found winter grasses beginning to sprout. The Bedouin rejoiced. Each family made individual short moves every few days, seeking the best grazing. Endless, joking arguments went on throughout the spring as each herdsman claimed himself the best Bedouin with the fattest camels.

Most of the northern tribesmen have sold their camels and now keep sheep and goats, depending on these for subsistence and for cash income from markets of the modern towns and cities. As we moved about with our camels, we often passed groups of three or four large tents— each, typically, with a small truck parked nearby. Most of the boys and a few of the girls of these families now study in new schools at the small oases that dot the area. Many of the young men have gone off to seek their fortunes in the oil fields or booming cities of Saudi Arabia and Kuwait. Nowadays, many spend only their holidays in the desert.

Whenever I visited the new oil towns I sought out these "modernized" youths. Most of them disliked the cities and felt estranged there. But they all eagerly pursued modern learning; many went to night school. They wanted to make money to send back to their families. All of them tried to maintain their communal way of life by sharing their housing, their evening meals, their leisure hours.

One of them told me: "You know, O my brother, the first thing we must never lose sight of in the cities is that we are *tribesmen* and that *all* the Āl Murrah are brothers. Our tents, our houses in the towns, whatever, are as one house. We owe absolute loyalty to each other because that is the custom of Arab tribesmen, of the *aṣīlīn*, the pure ones —those of pure descent."

My friend Rāshid ibn Ṭālib had to spend most of his days in the cities, much of it studying in the secondary school in Ad Dammām. Few of his fellow students came from Bedouin families, and he often felt alone in the classes. His people had always looked down on the cities as evil. The fathers and grandfathers of students bred in the towns and oases considered the Bedouin unkempt, rough, almost barbarian. These boys grew up fearing the desert and mistrusting the tribesmen. Most of Rāshid's classmates, nevertheless, respected him and praised his ability as a speaker and as a poet. They shared knowledge that none of their parents dreamed of.

Rāshid wanted his classmates to know the purity of the desert and

Shroudlike mask, burqu', *and cloak,* 'abāyah, *cover the face and head of a tribal woman. Tradition requires that girls assume the veil at puberty and wear it most of the time thereafter—even when sleeping; the gold-trimmed cloak can drop to the shoulders during a journey. Demure and polite, women eat apart from the men and keep to the* ḥarīm, *a sacrosanct part of the tent reserved solely for family life.*

once he invited some of them to visit his tents. He killed a sheep for them and feasted them generously, but a sense of strain pervaded the atmosphere. The town youths hardly spoke. No more than 20 or 30 miles from their homes, they found themselves in a completely alien environment. Rāshid tried to cheer things up by asking an old poet to recite some Bedouin poetry, but much of it referred condescendingly to the townspeople and recalled wars of the past against them. At last some of the students started discussing aspects of the history of World War II, and they and Rāshid and I got into a lively conversation—but it excluded the other Bedouin.

Life did not run easily for Rāshid in the cities. His tribesmen sought him out for advice and aid in their dealings with merchants or government officials. Emir Ṭālib often sent him as his representative to places all over eastern Arabia and to Iran. Sometimes I chided him for neglecting his studies, but he answered, "I am of the tribes, and I must work for their well-being even though it be something very minor."

Once we traveled together to the King Faisal Settlement Project. When its officials told Rāshid that they had enough underground water to support agriculture for at least one hundred years, Rāshid reasoned that one hundred years was a very short period of time in the history of his tribe. He thought that his people would do well to remember their skills of survival as nomads.

Rāshid and I went south, on another occasion, to a part of the Empty Quarter that he had never visited before. We intended to spend most of our time hunting, with Al Kurbī and Marzūq as guides, but Rāshid's relatives tied us down with invitations to meals in his honor. He loved the spontaneity of these kinsmen. Every night he sat up late telling stories from the *Thousand Nights and a Night* or reciting his own poems. All deeply respected his learning; he equally relished their stories of camels and daily life. Finally one night when we camped alone in the desert, he said, "I wish I could move my family, my mother and father and my own wife and children, away from the north near the cities to this area. Here alone can one find solitude and peace."

A difficult and unclear future awaits him, and he recognizes it. By warfare his father and grandfather led their tribes in the desert and made themselves felt in the cities. Their world crumbled when oil brought a new kind of economy into desert Arabia, and Rāshid knows that a modern chief must help his people adapt to new ways. He must represent them in the fast-changing world outside—and he must be able to advise them on every aspect of tradition.

I do not envy him his position. Few of his contemporaries understand it. His younger brother Sa'd, a boy in his late teens, once asked, "Why should one study? Rāshid has spent his whole life studying and he's not halfway content. He just mopes around the cities and never gets to enjoy any of the purity of the desert."

And Sa'd remarked to me once that any of his Bedouin cousins in the desert was much happier than anyone who went to the cities: "Why can't we just stay like that, all together, with our camels, with our brothers, with our God?"

Prized falcon perches alertly on the wrist of Mubārak, whose name means "blessed," near Al Ḥasā oasis. To the time-tried garb of loose robe and flowing headdress that shield the Bedouin against sun, wind-driven sand, and night-time chill, he adds a heavy armguard for protection against sharp talons. Deft killers of hare and bustard, falcons today provide sport for princes of eastern Arabia. Nomads, however, still depend on their own skills or those of saluki hounds to catch an occasional hare or gazelle. With rice, dates, and camel's milk as staples, the Āl Murrah normally eat little meat. Below, desert faces peer from the past and look to the future. Foamy camel's milk splotches the face of a smiling boy. For the everyday red-and-white ghuṭrah of the tribe, Al Kurbī substitutes a lighter-weight white headdress; as his friend the author (second from right) savors the smoke from burning sandalwood, the fine white fabric concentrates its fragrance. A young man slings his rifle in the customary muzzle-first manner. Two elders, their faces chiseled by years in a harsh but well-loved environment, show contentment with life in the Empty Quarter.

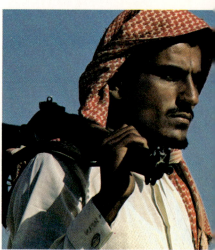

THOMAS J. ABERCROMBIE, N.G.S. STAFF (BELOW)

In the cool of morning, a Bajau father and son pole their lipa—houseboat—toward a moorage in the coastal shallow

Gentle People of Gentle Seas, the
BAJAU Still Roam Philippine Water

By H. Arlo Nimmo, Ph.D.
Illustrations by David R. Bridge, National Geographic Staff

f the Tawitawi Islands. If the wind favors them, they can roll up the lipa's roof of palm matting and hoist a sail.

Boat-dwelling

DAWN PROMISED to pass into a rather empty day. High tide bobbed the houseboats of the Bajau moorage to a dying breeze. I sat at the stern of my own houseboat, idly smoking and watching the activities of the floating village. For a year I had been in Sulu Province of the Republic of the Philippines, conducting anthropological research among the boat-dwelling Bajau of the Tawitawi Islands for my Ph.D. dissertation. Sailing with them on glinting waters, I had shared many things—and almost given up hope on others.

The houseboat of Masarani, my favorite Bajau friend, lay some 30 feet from mine. He stepped onto the deck and greeted me as he, too, gazed around. Like most Bajau men, he had hair bleached auburn from long hours of fishing in the sun; his smile revealed teeth blackened from chewing betel nut. Only a pair of shorts covered his lean, dark body, now stretched taut as he yawned widely. I met Masarani during my first month in Sulu, when small children ran away crying at my approach and women, equally suspicious of a white stranger, went to their boats. Even men generally found an excuse to leave my company, but Masarani and I soon became close friends. As I shared in the fishing, ceremonies of birth and death, and daily tediousness of living, our friendship deepened into mutual respect.

Musulaini, Masarani's wife, came onto the deck and shouted a greeting. She tied a turban around her head—women guard the beauty of their dark hair. Two of her sisters paddled up in a small dugout. She stepped into it with her 7-year-old son; they planned to collect firewood from nearby beaches. Masarani would spend the morning at home, watching the other four children, mending nets or repairing the houseboat, the *lipa*. Other men of the village loaded nets and spears into dugouts for a day of fishing.

A young mother and her daughter smiled at me as they paddled by in a boat laden with cassava acquired from the nearby village of landdwellers; they would spend the day peeling the tubers, grating them to pulp, and squeezing out the toxic juices, preparing for the evening meal. As always, songs punctuated the moorage: lullabies to fussy babies, jaunty love ballads from infatuated teen-agers, happy children's songs from the exposed reef, the community playground.

Some families, leaving for fishing trips or visits to other moorages, poled their boats to deep water where they took down the matting roofs to unfurl sails. Boats arriving from elsewhere pulled down sails and poled through the shallows in search of kinsmen and friends. I took my morning count of houseboats: 45, typical of Tungbangkao.

Masarani stepped into a small dugout and began paddling in my direction. "Where are you going?" he asked, a traditional greeting. "Nowhere," I replied in Samal, his language. "Are you going fishing?" "Not today. I am resting from fishing."

Well he deserved it, I thought. We had been fishing almost steadily ever since we left Tungkalang, our home moorage 25 miles to the

Inside a Bajau house, an infant wrapped for a nap gazes from a sarong tied into a buahan, *or hammock-cradle. Rice-flour paste, a common cosmetic, whitens the mother's face and arms. Although some Bajau have built small houses on stilts at the five traditional moorages, many abandon these fixed dwellings and return to their houseboats whenever the need—or wish— to move strikes them.*

N.G.S. PHOTOGRAPHER DEAN CONGER

Currently teaching anthropology at California State College, Hayward, H. ARLO NIMMO reports on 24 months of research among the Bajau.

Light breezes urge a fishing party on its way. The men have sewn rice-flour sacks into a sail for the **dapang**. It tows a **boggoh** lashed to its stern; the boggoh may also see use as the keel of a houseboat. Superb fishermen, these people know from youth the cycles of shifting winds, tides, currents, and schools of fish. "Throughout seemingly featureless expanses of water," says the author, "they pinpoint precise locations that they recognize by name, much as land-dwellers know the streets around their homes." At right, an old man churns the water with a shark rattle made of pierced coconut shells strung onto a bamboo frame; he hopes this will attract sharks within range of his spear. "It works," the author reports. Below, two men bring in their weighted nylon gill net —empty—in the course of an evening's reef fishing. The Bajau also use hooks and lines, and occasionally explode dynamite in the water, an illegal practice, to stun the fish —whatever will produce the best results.

NATIONAL GEOGRAPHIC PHOTOGRAPHER DEAN CONGER (ABOVE)

Seated in a dugout tied to a houseboat, women grate peeled cassava exchanged by a farmer for fish. On her head each wears a hos—a garment that also serves men as a loincloth and women as a robe or skirt. Below, a Bajau matron stirs a pot of fish boiling on a clay hearth near

NATIONAL GEOGRAPHIC PHOTOGRAPHER DEAN CONGER (BELOW)

her buff water jug. She grows kitchen herbs in the miniature canoe hanging outside the lipa.

west, ten days ago. As he came aboard, I offered him a cigarette, which he accepted.

"I talked to Hadjulani this morning" — his brother-in-law, a member of our fishing group. "We have decided to take you to see the *tahu-tahu.*" I nearly choked on my cigarette. For almost a year I had asked Masarani to take me to Sangasiapu, the small island where his people keep wooden anthropomorphic figures which they believe to contain evil spirits. Always there had been excuses. It was too far away. The seas were too rough. There was not time. Sangasiapu Island housed such great evil that I would probably fall ill and die.

Before I could speak, Masarani continued: "You have been good to us, have given us much medicine. We are thankful and want to help you all we can. The island is near, so we have decided to take you if you want to go." I assured him I was ready at any time.

"I have told you before that it is very dangerous for you," began the familiar lecture. "You are not accustomed to our spirits and do not know how to behave properly before them." Again he warned of the hazards that awaited me. I said I understood and would write a letter absolving him of any responsibility for misfortunes. He told a sister-in-law of our plan — she would keep the children.

"We must first go to the boat of Hadjulani." I grabbed my camera and notebook and stepped into the dugout. Within minutes we were in Hadjulani's houseboat.

Its interior was dark. The keel was made from a log dugout, planked to form a hull about 30 feet long and 6 feet wide. Additional planks made the deck on which we sat. The roof of woven nipa-palm matting covered a house area about 20 feet long but only 4 feet high at the gable.

Hadjira, Hadjulani's wife, took down the mat at the stern and lifted the small clay cooking hearth out into the open. She started a driftwood fire and placed a pot of fish over it. The four children were still sleeping, wrapped in their sarongs and curled together for warmth on their mats. Although I always felt somewhat cramped in Hadjulani's boat, his home was more spacious than many. One family I knew — a man, his wife, and three small children — had a living space of 6 feet by 4.

Hadjulani announced that ritual must be conducted to ask the tahu-tahu spirits to refrain from their normal evil. He lighted incense and the three of us held our hands, palms upward, on our crossed legs as he asked the spirits to allow our safe passage. Then we sprinkled a fragrant tonic over our hands and faces, while he told me that on Sangasiapu I should not laugh, shout, spit or otherwise relieve myself, break branches from the trees, or look over my shoulder. Finally in a small dugout we paddled into the morning.

The dazzling early light revealed the familiar sea world of the Bajau, the Sulu Archipelago. Its tiny islands stretch like scattered gems from a brilliant emerald chain across the azure sea between Mindanao and the great island of Borneo. The Sulu Sea rolls to the north, the Celebes Sea to the south. Both are protectively surrounded by islands and consequently are among the gentlest on earth.

Sea and land alike provide for Sulu's people. The land-dwellers till

Masarani, the author's closest friend among the Bajau, prepares to moor his houseboat to a stake driven firmly into the coral reef at the northwest tip of Bilatan Island. Branches of driftwood at the stern make a convenient rack for drying garments, nets, or fish in the hot sun.

small plots of cassava, dry rice, and vegetables; they harvest coconuts for copra, chief export of the archipelago. Some fishermen also keep small gardens, but many trade their fresh fish for vegetables and sell dried catches to Chinese fish-buyers of the towns and villages.

The land-dwelling people, Tausug and Samal, are Moslems; they consider the Bajau mere pagans who have yet to embrace Islamic culture. Although the Samal are reluctant to admit it, they are very closely related to the Bajau, who number about 12,000 all told. The Tausug speak a different language, are culturally distinct, and are concentrated around Jolo Island, northeast of Tawitawi.

Unique among the peoples of Sulu are the 1,600 boat-dwelling Bajau of the Tawitawi group, who spend their entire lives upon the sea. Among five moorages in the islands, they ply the waters in their small houseboats as regularly and persistently as the fishes themselves.

As we paddled across the glasslike surface, Masarani and Hadjulani spoke further of the Bajau spirit world. "These spirits on Sangasiapu are not of our people," explained Masarani. "That is why they are so evil. Our spirits, *ummagged,* once lived among us. They know what hard lives we lead and do not harm us unless we anger them. But the tahu-tahu spirits are like the land people. They do not like us; they are pleased to make us ill or even cause us death."

Spirits are everywhere—land, sea, and sky—but prefer certain islands that the Bajau avoid. Sangasiapu is one, famous as the receptor of tahu-tahu (the name covers spirit and carving alike).

I had seen the healing ceremony several times. In a simple rite, a shaman coaxes the disease-causing spirit to leave the body of the afflicted and enter a tahu-tahu carved for the occasion. Then the shaman takes the tahu-tahu to its island and deposits it in the limbs of a special tree. Now, without enthusiasm, my friends were taking me to the site.

As we pulled our boat onto the beach, they told me it was time to observe the tabus. Masarani gave me an *anting-anting,* a shiny black stone, to carry for further protection. We followed a well-worn path into dense tropical foliage. Periodically, Masarani silently stopped to leave food and incense for the temperamental spirits. Soon we arrived at a small clearing. At its center stood a tree about 25 feet tall, gnarled, twisted, dense. Masarani nodded—this was the end of our quest.

The scientific world view of my own culture took flight, as I sensed the foreboding evil of the place. The tree held about 30 tahu-tahu. Some had been there many years; the growth of the tree had nearly devoured them. Dozens of small green and white flags—the spirits' favorite colors—were scattered on the limbs as offerings. Leaves rustled to the quick movements of bright green lizards about a foot long. Beyond the trees the sea murmured restlessly.

Recalling my own role, I took out my camera. My companions glared in disapproval, but I made a dozen shots and jotted down notes: shamans obviously carve in haste, many figures crude; some slender, some squat; scratched-in lines may indicate features and limbs, others modeled in detail; length varies, three feet to less than a foot; sex clear in some, not all; a very few painted.

Half an hour later I indicated that I was ready to leave. They had been ready for some time. We kept silence until we were paddling away.

"You see," I said, "the spirits were not offended." The men said nothing. That evening I had a severe attack of dysentery and the next day I accidentally dropped my camera into the sea, spoiling the film. The men answered then: Without doubt, the tahu-tahu were punishing me for my trespass. Never again could I talk the men into taking me to Sangasiapu—partly, perhaps, because there was a noticeable lack of insistence in my requests. Our voyages took us elsewhere.

The Bajau move continually, but not as aimless wanderers. Their movements are patterned, predictable, and undertaken for very real reasons. The moon is their calendar. Its phases determine tides and currents; these affect the movements of fish. The Bajau move accordingly to exploit the various fishing grounds.

Ceremonies also determine many voyages. Kinsmen attend one another's ceremonies of healing, circumcision, and marriage; a rite at one of the five major moorages attracts people from the others. A death means that an entourage of mourners must travel to one of the two cemetery islands for the burial; and religion demands that sea folk regularly visit the graves of relatives.

Often a houseboat calls at an island for drinking water and firewood, or for cassava and other produce that farmers trade for fish. Rarely does a boat remain at one moorage as long as a month.

Among intricate channels through reefs and rocks, with tricky currents, the Bajau make their way with certainty. They know specific locations in the waters by name, learning sea ways from infancy.

A Bajau nomad spends much of his life isolated with his wife and children in their houseboat. At intervals, however, married siblings and their families travel together for a couple of weeks, cooperating in certain types of fishing and enjoying companionship.

Kinship ties and tradition designate a major moorage as "home," and a family often joins kinsmen there. Each moorage has several such kinship groups and recognizes an elder as headman. His power is very limited; he serves as an arbitrator in the event of quarrels within the moorage. Bajau society is extremely egalitarian, and no person or family ever amasses much power or wealth from the sea.

Most Bajau fish every day, but I had to wait some time to try shark fishing, one of the most exciting techniques and the most dangerous.

Masarani told me one evening that we would go the next morning. Day dawned steely gray. Beyond the moorage reef I could see whitecaps. I joined Masarani in his houseboat and hopefully asked, "Is the sea too rough?" He replied that it was perfect. After a quick breakfast of cold cassava and dried fish, he collected his gear from under the deck and placed it in a 12-foot dugout.

We each took a paddle and before long the swells at the edge of the reef were tossing our boat. Masarani announced that we needed fresh fish for bait, and slipped over the side with a spear. Within 15 minutes we had fish enough for bait—and for dinner if we missed our shark.

We paddled farther into the heaving swells. One moment we were surveying the sea range from atop a mountain of water, the next we were deep in a valley surrounded by walls of sea. We reached an area that seemed to me no different from the seas we had just passed.

Then Masarani said sharks were nearby. We placed our paddles in the boat, and I was told not to talk without absolute necessity. He took two steel hooks, about ten inches long, baited them, and set one at the bow and one at the stern, fastening the lines securely to the boat. He took up a shark rattle, a stick frame with half a dozen dried coconut shells, lowered it into the water, and shook it as he began singing in a slow, melancholy voice to the *datu*, the chieftain: "I am shaking my rattle to call you. I know you are under my boat, waiting to take my bait. Come now and take my bait and hook, Datu Shark. Your fin is handsome and looks like a flag in the sea. . . ."

Within minutes a fin appeared about 20 feet away and began to move toward the hook at my end of the boat. Masarani continued to shake the rattle and sing. The shark came closer: a hammerhead that looked as long as the dugout. Masarani whispered that as soon as it struck the hook, we should change positions quickly so he could finish it off. I nodded. The shark circled us a couple of times and then, without warning, attacked the hook at Masarani's end.

Masarani rammed his spear into the giant fish's head and began beating it with a heavy wooden club. I frantically bailed the water that the dying shark was thrashing into our frail craft.

While Masarani pounded the shark's head in a bloody cloud of sea, I noticed two more fins, and yelled a warning. He told me to pull in my hook and help him lift the now-inert shark into the boat. After a couple of failures I speared the tail and pulled the shark to the dugout. As Masarani struggled with the head I lifted the tail. We almost had our catch aboard when it gave one last desperate writhe. I dropped the tail and almost fell into the sea after it. Masarani kept his hold and told me to get the tail again—the other sharks were approaching. With a burst of strength we wrestled the great dead fish into the boat. None too soon, for the two sharks were now frantically searching about us for the source of that fresh blood. We quietly waited until the blood-cloud dispersed and the sharks departed before we paddled toward the hazy strip of darkness in the distance—the moorage, and safety.

Death strikes often among the Bajau. Its agents include tuberculosis, dysentery, difficult childbirth, and infected wounds from fishing accidents. The Bajau rarely consult the doctors in the port town of Bongao, fearing and misunderstanding medical techniques. Always they bury the dead in their own cemeteries. Burial elsewhere is unthinkable to the Bajau, who consistently told me the bones of their people should not be scattered—a tradition that always struck me as ironic for people who spend all their days scattered in small, isolated groups over the seas of Tawitawi.

About six months after I arrived in Sulu, I went on a fishing journey with Masarani, his family, two of his brothers-in-law, and their families. We had been out for a week when he said we would sail the next day for the moorage at Tungbangkao. *(Continued on page 88)*

Wielding a torch of coconut fronds, a woman burns algae and marine worms off her husband's dugout at Tungkalang, a moorage at the southwest corner of Sanga Sanga Island. On the beach nearby, a new boat begins to take shape as a skilled boatmaker swings a patuk, *an adzlike tool with interchangeable blades.*

Balancing on homemade stilts, boys stride through the shallows. Nearby, youngsters from several families play together on the porch of a house; living in crowded quarters fosters close family ties. His hair bleached by sun and salt, a youth (above) comforts his wailing sister. She wears strands of plastic beads to ward off saitan, malevolent spirits feared by the Bajau.

Overleaf: Waiting for the
sun to chase the chill of
night, a sleepy matron sits
in the bow of a lipa moored
near Bajau houses at Tungkalang. A dugout with
built-up plank sides, the
vessel has walls of woven
palm fronds. Bongao
Mountain, a landmark
visible far at sea, looms
across the Sanga Sanga
Channel to the south.

N.G.S. PHOTOGRAPHER DEAN CONGER

It was late afternoon. Men were sitting in the prows of their boats chatting about the day's fishing while women cooked the evening meal.
Children played on the nearby beach, and I caught up on my journal.
Then we noticed houseboats off to the wést. Masarani thought the lead
boat belonged to his sister's husband, Lanipuddin, and decided to
catch up with the flotilla. We collected the children, lifted anchor,
and set out.

Over the evening waters drifted the sound of drums and gongs, and
a faint chant: a funeral chant. As we came up we learned who had died.

Lanipuddin, said his brother, became ill four days ago. He came
home from fishing with sharp pains in his lower right abdomen. His
wife gave him a herbal concoction but in the night he felt even greater
pains, so she sent for Laisiha, an old female shaman. Laisiha found
out that Lanipuddin, to collect bark for caulking his boat, had foolishly
gone to a small islet inhabited by particularly malevolent spirits.
Laisiha diagnosed the case: The spirits had resented the trespass and
were punishing the intruder. The old woman said prayers and offered
incense, and even called in other shamans to assist—but all to no
avail. Lanipuddin died in a violent fever. The funeral party was now
en route to the burial island of Bunabunaan, to moor for the night.

SALAPUDDIN, our host, invited us into the funeral boat. His
brother's body, wrapped in a white shroud, lay surrounded by
women chanting words of sorrow and comfort to the deceased.
Members of our party joined them. Masarani began: "You were my
brother-in-law; my best friend. When you were alive, we often fished
together. You were always generous and always gave away more fish
than you kept. How shall we continue to live now that you are gone?"

And Masarani's wife: "You were the best brother-in-law anyone
could have. You were always kind to your wife and your children. We
will remember you the rest of our lives, and cry each time we remember."

Their grief ran deep; but if a Bajau does not mourn properly at a
funeral, the spirit of the dead will visit him with misfortune.

At dawn we poled the houseboats in to Bunabunaan. We approached
with some reserve since the ummagged hover about their graves. In
addition, a neighboring island is a rendezvous for *saitan*. The saitan
never lived as humans but demand cautious treatment. Both types are
generally indifferent to men, but occasionally they cause bad luck or
illness or unusually stormy weather. Then they must be placated with
prayers and small offerings of betel, rice, or cigarettes.

When we anchored, all the men but a couple of elders went ashore
to prepare the grave at a family vault. Beneath a simple roof, carvings
of stylized human figures, fish and flower forms, and ornate prows
from houseboats serve as grave markers on the vaults. Under them a
layer of sand covers boards that close the grave itself. The men cleared
and opened a grave, examining offerings left with past burials and
picking up bones that called past kinsmen to mind. This was not at
all hushed or sacred; in fact there was a good deal of subdued laughing
and joking among those not intimately related to the deceased.

Then women brought Lanipuddin's clothing, his box for betel, and his fishing gear. Neatly packaged, these were placed in the grave.

We returned for the body, and the entire group of chanting mourners accompanied Lanipuddin to his rest. A shaman placed incense at his head with a final prayer that he not harm the survivors who had properly mourned and buried his body. Men of the family covered the grave again and placed on it a small boat Lanipuddin had owned. The shaman poured a libation of fresh water and asked the deceased to bless the living with good health and fortune. The widow stepped forward and chanted, weeping: "You are alone, but do not fear. I cannot live here without you. Soon I shall come to you."

We returned to the boats, spoke a few words of parting, went our separate sea ways. That afternoon Masarani and I fished; that evening we sat at the prow of the boat. At the stern Musulaini cleared away the latest meal. The children had dropped off to sleep. We smoked quietly and watched the spreading crimson of a spectacular sunset.

"We were like brothers," Masarani said, looking into the sunset.

"I know. I'm sorry," I replied.

"I don't know why we die. I don't know why we live. Sometimes it seems I know nothing." He flipped his cigarette into the sea and retired to the interior of the boat. I continued to look into the darkening reds of the sunset, and thought of Masarani's comments. Man's eternal questions. And as the sunset died, and the blackness of the tropical night descended, it seemed they would remain forever eternal as the sea.

Next morning we resumed our journey. A breeze encouraged us to unfurl the sails. As we approached Tungbangkao we heard drums and gongs again — the happy, tinkling music of a Bajau wedding.

Masarani told me that his nephew was marrying a first cousin, a proper and desirable Bajau match. Some weeks earlier Masarani, like all the groom's kinsmen, had contributed to the bride-price of 60 pesos — about $15. The bride's family spent it on the celebration.

We had come late. The previous day and night, the families of the bride and groom had entertained the entire moorage on the beach. Music and dancing had honored the young couple. But we saw the actual ceremony. As we poled our way to the houseboat of the groom's parents, a chair was placed at the prow. A shaman led the sad-looking bride, about 15, out of the crowd and seated her there. He poured seawater over her and chanted prayers for her good health, happiness, good fortune, and fertility. Then women of the groom's family took her into the shadowy interior to change into a brilliant yellow sateen blouse and a burgundy sarong. Her attendants decked her out in all the family ornaments — mostly costume jewelry.

The bride steadfastly continued to look like the unhappiest person at the moorage — in keeping with etiquette. White *borak*, a paste of oil and rice flour, was caked over her face; her eyebrows and hairline were outlined in black; bright-red lipstick was thick on her mouth. Her elaborate headdress incorporated costume jewelry, crepe paper, and — it seemed — any bright-colored object available.

Gongs and drums played while the groom's prospective in-laws helped him with a similar but less elaborate toilette. When all was ready, a shaman led him to the boat where his bride awaited. As he arrived, two older women held up a sarong to hide her.

The shaman sat down with the groom and the fathers of the couple. Over burning incense he prayed to the deceased kinsmen of both families and asked them to visit the young couple with good fortune and many children. Then he tapped at the sarong that hid the bride, as if at a door. After some joking, the women dropped the sarong and revealed the lovely girl in all her finery. Music resumed, and the bridegroom took a seat next to his bride.

A few minutes later, the newlyweds went to the stern of the boat and a male in-law carried each through the shallows to shore, where there was room for dancing. Mats were spread for the couple to sit on as spectators and musicians crowded around. After several minutes of music, the bride stood up and briefly danced the graceful, stylized *angigal*. When she sat down, the groom rose and danced a few steps in similar fashion. When he sat down, the music stopped. The wedding had ended. Husband and wife went to the boat of her parents, while others dismantled the decorations or turned to afternoon routine.

Our party returned to the town of Bongao, to sell dried fish accumulated on the trip. Masarani wanted to dry-dock his boat to recaulk a seam. And Hadjulani was anxious to get home; his wife would soon give birth, and she wanted her mother to deliver the child.

A week later, before dawn at Tungkalang, Hadjira bore a son with her mother as midwife, two of her sisters and an aged male shaman in attendance. Hadjulani came to my boat and proudly told me the name of his new son would be Englisani because he wanted the baby to become a man who spoke English and lived like an American.

Most likely Englisani will lead a life very different from that of his parents. The government of the Philippines has strengthened order in the archipelago, long troubled with lawlessness; and the unwarlike Bajau are beginning to leave their remote reefs and enjoy security on land. Some become commercial fishermen, dealing with the Chinese merchants, and display their wealth by building a house. The Roman Catholic mission school at Bongao influences some to try Western customs. Although born in a boat, Englisani will probably grow up in a house. At the mission school he will learn to read and write. He may not even be a fisherman. He may have gardens and a copra plantation on one of the Tawitawi Islands. He will undoubtedly be a Christian or a Moslem like his land-dwelling neighbors, not a pagan like his sea-roaming nomad ancestors.

As dawn revealed the shadowy forms of the houseboats, I realized that in twenty years the moorage might well be a village of houses. Perhaps a few boat-dwellers would cling to the old ways. Exotic people who wandered the seas in quaint lipas may become subjects for romantic stories told to children and visitors. For new winds of change have reached Tawitawi, and as the Bajau so often told me, "Even the shaman cannot stop the winds."

Dressed in their best, girls perform an angigal, *or ceremonial dance, aboard a lipa. Such graceful gestures celebrate important occasions—even some funerals. At the cemetery on Bunabunaan Island (below) stand carefully painted family grave shelters. Bajau believe they must give proper burial rites or* ummagged, *spirits of the dead, may bring bad luck, illness, or death. Against the uncertainties of Westernization, the Bajau know no defense. To help lessen its shocks, the Oblate Fathers operate schools for Bajau children. Father Emile Laquerre ferries one of his students from Bongao to her home at Tungkalang.*

Sixty days on the track, a young Qashqā'ī family plods the last lap of the fall migration to grazing areas near t

Hardy Shepherds of Iran's Zāgros
QASHQĀ'Ī Build a Future Through Tent

By Mohammad Bahmanbegui

Illustrations by Roland and Sabrina Michaud

ROLAND MICHAUD

rsian Gulf. *They have herded goats and sheep 300 miles from mountain pastures, and will return in spring.*

Mountains,
chool Education

Tehrān

Zágros Mountains

Isfahan

Semirom

Ābādeh

IRAQ

Shīrāz

IRAN

Khonj

Persian

Gulf

Swirls of dust followed my jeep as it bounced along the rocky track. I was now more than 300 miles northwest of Shīrāz, crossing a succession of rises in one of the plains spreading between the sharp stone ridges of the Zāgros Mountains of Iran. For miles I had seen nothing on these hot, dry expanses except the peaks rimming the tableland, an occasional village of one- or two-room mud houses, tan like the earth, and a few black rectangles of Qashqā'ī* tribesmen's tents, menaced only by wandering columns of whirling dust devils.

Then I saw ahead under the cloudless bright sky a patch of green, the one I was looking for. My brother Nader in his big tent at that grove of trees would be watching for my dust clouds, like smoke signals. I smiled with pleasure to picture our numerous cousins running from their tents to Nader's when they heard his shout.

Even before I came to a full stop by the long row of guy ropes—each trimmed with a large red, blue, or green tassel—steadying the poles along the open front of Nader's tent, I was reaching out of the jeep to clasp hands with my relatives. Their wide grins matched in jauntiness the turned-up flaps of their tan felt tribal hats.

"Khōshgalling! Welcome!" Nader said in the first language I learned as a child, the Turkish dialect of the Qashqā'ī. And then he added in Persian, our national language, "Qadam bar cheshm! Your foot up in my eye!" This means, "I like your coming so much, I'd feel happy even if you kicked me in the eye!"

Nader's wife Shahnaz came hurrying around the corner of the long tent. She pulled at a filmy white mantle, a sarandāz, held by a purple scarf around the crown of her head—though Moslem, our women go unveiled. The hem of her full and shimmering red skirt danced to her quick steps. "Salām! Hello! You've finally come!" she said. "We'll kill a lamb to roast and we have partridges on the skewers ready to cook for kebab. Nader shot them this morning."

Of course all my relatives knew I had come on business. As head of Tribal Education for Iran, I give examinations to the children of the tent schools, white portable umbrellas with no furniture or equipment except a blackboard propped up on two sticks. "Where is Fazel, the teacher?" I asked.

"He's bringing the tent," Nader answered. "Come sit down and have a glass of tea." We sat cross-legged on the brightly patterned Qashqā'ī rugs covering the tent floor, and leaned against a 40-foot-long mound of goods and supplies covered with beautiful handwoven carpet-cloths. My cousin Ali started a small fire in a shallow hole just outside the tent, and brought out pot, glasses, and sugar lumps broken from a long loaf.

Arriving at Kohnarcheh, ten miles west of Semirom, always gives me the feeling of coming home. Many of my earliest memories center on this summer campsite of my family. I recall, for example, my joy and

*Most authorities now prefer "Qashqā'ī" to the older English renderings "Kashgai" or "Gashgai." Each syllable is stressed: "khosh-khy-ee."

Director of Iran's Office of Tribal Education, MOHAMMAD BAHMANBEGUI *writes of the nomadic life he has lived—and has profoundly changed.*

ROLAND MICHAUD

*Palming a fresh spin to each wooden spindle as it swings into reach,
a 10-year-old girl plies yarn for rug-making. Two strands of wool
run to each spindle. Rugs bring in a third of the income of some families.*

KAZEM AHMADI

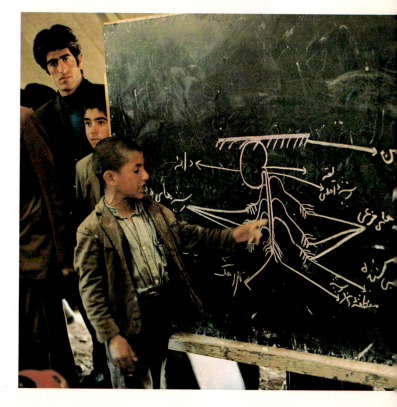

Poised fifth-grader explains water
and air pressure to classmates
and relatives at a demonstration
by tribal students. At right, an
intent fourth-grader describes
how a seed sprouts. Impatiently
awaiting her turn, a pupil displays a card listing topics she
can discuss for visiting examiner
Mohammad Bahmanbegui, found-
er and guiding spirit of Iran's
tent-school program. A thousand
tents like the one at left, each
with some 25 eager students in
grades one through six, dot tribal
grazing areas in winter and summer.

ROLAND MICHAUD (ABOVE); SABRINA MICHAUD

In their open-front tent at summer camp in the Zāgros Mountains, the family of a prosperous onetime tribal chief dines from a cloth laid on fine Qashqā'ī rugs. A teen-age daughter prefers West-ern clothes. Covered with a jājīm, or carpet-cloth, a mound of household goods stretches the 60-foot length of the tent; bedding lies on top. In most—and far more mod-est—tents, men usually eat separately. Women tend to their chores: roll-ing out thin sheets of dough and draping them on a hot griddle; testing hanks of newly dyed rug yarn for dryness.

relief when as a four-year-old, tied for safety to a horse and saddle nearly every day for two months during our spring migration, I saw in the distance our little hill and its few scattered poplars. Tricklets of spring water run through short grass near the tent and down the slope toward the rocky bed of a brook. How many times have I stooped to wash my hands and look out toward our three towering colored moun-tains, all part of the Zāgros range. Āq Dāgh of whitish rock stands to the east; Goy Dāgh, green with shrubs and grass in spring, rises in the west; in the north looms Qara Dāgh, stony black.

Scores of green spots like Kohnarcheh—usually owned by Qashqā'ī families of considerable prosperity and standing—brighten these mon-otone highland plains. In the past, ownership of vast acreage here gave great economic and some measure of political power to the *Kad-khodās,* or clan chieftains; the *Kalāntars,* or those hereditary chiefs above the Kadkhodās; and especially to the *Khāns,* or hereditary lead-ers of the five tribes of the Qashqā'ī.

And in order to preserve this power, these tribal leaders used to arm themselves and their peoples.

But during the last two decades, beginning in the early 1950's, the disarmament of Iranian tribes, the distribution of land, and the na-tionalization of pastures have changed all this. Now loaded guns no longer stand in every Qashqā'ī tent, to be used against the government or neighboring tribes. Now much of the Khāns' vast lands and numer-ous villages with their farms have been parceled out by the govern-ment to individual families, village peasants or nomadic tribesmen.

Onetime tribal nobles or their families drive jeeps and trucks from their houses in Shīrāz or Kāzerūn or Firūzābād to the Zāgros to pass the summer in the cooler climate. While their wheat and barley crops mature on their southern farms with citrus and date orchards, they tend apple trees and vegetables on their northern land, watered by springs or deep wells, and send their hundreds of sheep and goats to nearby grasslands. They have no official role, but act as spokesmen for and still have some influence among their people—a fact officials make use of in administering tribal affairs.

Within some miles of Nader's green hill, about 50 families of the Bahman-Beg-lu clan of the Amaleh tribe live in scattered groups of tents. Like most of the other 25,000 Qashqā'ī families, they depend on free grazing for their animals. Their herds average about 70 animals, with perhaps 40 sheep and 30 goats, both of which supply meat as well as milk for making cheese, yogurt, and butter. The sheep also yield wool and the goats the long, black hair woven into tentcloth.

I can look at the size of a Qashqā'ī tent, the number and quality of rugs in it, the height and length of the mound of baggage piled neatly at the back, the richness of the cloth in the women's attire—and how far their skirts stand out with petticoats—and give a close estimate of family income.

Inevitably, with every move of the government to modernize and develop Iran, good grazing lands have shrunk. Roads constructed in the pasture areas have cut into the grass. The sprawling, smoking

SABRINA MICHAUD

Sequin-adorned Shahla, sitting before a reed screen in her family's tent, wears no veil— although a Moslem —and does her hair in the favorite Qashqā'ī style. Daughter of a former Khān with many servants, she spends much time on her clothes, looking to the day when relatives will arrange a marriage for her. Since 1960, some tribal families have let daughters become tent-school teachers, a revolutionary change.

cement factory at Shīrāz blocks a top-grade migration route; gardens and grain fields of village farmers stretch out across more and more traditional pastures of the tent-dwelling Qashqā'ī.

All this, added to the devastating effects of frequent years of drought, has made nomadic shepherding less and less able to feed millions of sheep and goats and hundreds of thousands of pack animals. I believe, in fact, that within 25 years the migratory way of life will end for most of my people.

I once thought settlement might mean the end of the Qashqā'ī themselves, for how could they—illiterate and untrained, often not speaking Persian—make a living on poor pastures and survive in houses far less healthful than nomadic tents?

I tried during the 1950's to find some way to help them survive, physically, economically, and perhaps even culturally. I had returned to my tribe some years before from Tehrān, where I had completed a law degree. As the eldest son and successor of the leader of the little Bahman-Beg-lu clan, I had enough income to enable me to enjoy the leisurely outdoor life. I had my purebred horses, my hunting dogs, my guns, my games with friends. I liked the life of the open tent.

But I saw my poorer relatives walking miles to have letters read or written for them, or getting into difficulties because they couldn't read or understand regulations and instructions. I began to teach those close at hand to read and write. Then I taught their neighbors when they came and asked me to, and then neighbors from farther off.

As droughts and loss of land hurt worse, I saw that giving education was the best way to work for a better future for my people. I started a class for older children in 1952, in the shade of our traditional white guest tent. When the families moved to grassier spots, the tent was folded and taken along. I found I could teach them to read and write in Persian as a second language in the eight months of summer and winter camp. With eager requests of the tribesmen for more schools, I asked the officials to help me.

At this critical point, I was able to rely upon three sources of aid. The government contributed to the training of the teachers, the Americans through their Point Four Program helped with supplies, and the tribal people themselves paid the teachers' salaries. It was a good beginning, but shaky, depending upon three temporary sources. After four very difficult and uncertain years, our work was manifest. Under the guidance of H.I.M. Shahanshah of Iran, the government agreed to pay for a formal tribal educational system. And shortly thereafter, as a result of a visit to four tribal schools near Shīrāz by His Imperial Majesty, the Ministry of Education made an even greater commitment to the project. From no schools at all, the Qashqā'ī and other tribes in Fārs Province, empire center of ancient Persia, had by 1970 a thousand classes under white tents. Each offers instruction through the sixth grade. Four hundred more tent classes have moved to buildings serving about 5,000 families who have settled during that time.

With the deepest satisfaction, I have heard foreign observers praise our tribal schools. And I would like to think that our success comes in part from my having lived, boy and man, as a tribesman, knowing and loving the life and the people.

Until I was 13, I lived only in a tent. During five months of winter, we camped near Khonj on a grassy knoll much like the one at Kohnarcheh. Here, some hundred miles from the Persian Gulf, each day men and boys tended the animals, rode horses, practiced shooting, made tea, went hunting in the hills for the male ibex, gazelles, mouflon, and partridges. Women and girls spun wool even when they went walking, wove rugs for their own tents and for sale, milked goats and made cheese or yogurt, and baked thin sheets of bread, *nān*, on campfire griddles.

Then with the flowering month of Farvardīn, the feasting, present-giving, and visiting on March 21—Persian New Year, or *Nō-Rūz*—gave formal notice that tender new grass was sprouting in the north, far from the rising heat and dryness of the south. Sheep and goats were sheared, and one morning stakes were pulled, tents folded, bags and boxes tied onto donkeys and camels. Singing and full of hope, the Qashqā'ī began their journey happy to see the animals fatten as they ate their way to summer camps in the Zāgros. Some clans would travel nearly 150 miles, others more, our clan about 300 miles.

Every bend in the track, every hill, pass, ravine, every watering place I knew. I saw nothing of towns except once a year. Then, as the migration took us close to Shīrāz, my mother rode with me on horseback to the holy Shi'ah Moslem shrine of Shāh Cherāgh. I learned to read and write because my father, leader of 200 families, hired a secretary to read and write for him—and teach me.

Now I come by jeep from Shīrāz to the summer camps, visiting tent schools where *all* Qashqā'ī children can get an education. Schools are scattered over 30,000 square miles and most of them I can reach only by rough track. Sometimes I find myself asking children to work arithmetic problems by lantern light.

Sipping tea under Nader's tent, I saw Fazel and a swarm of children setting up the pole of the tent school. I was eager to go to them, but my brother was speaking anxiously about the autumn migration. "You know this has been the driest year we have ever seen. At Nō-Rūz when we started the move north, no flowers bloomed, grass hardly came up, and we were too worried to sing."

I did know. The normal rainy season brings about 13 inches of water. In a bad season, we have four or five inches. In 1970 a mere three inches —less than in the Sahara—fell on some parts of Fārs. Only because we had 15 inches in 1969 could even a little grass grow.

Nader went on. "Summer heat has shriveled the grassy stubs here in the high plains, and cold will soon menace our flocks. We need to start south now, where perhaps a little rain will bring some winter grass. But the Gendarmerie captain for the Amaleh tribe told me we're scheduled to wait three more weeks. So little grass will be left on the track that we will have to buy barley to feed the animals for a whole month, or else kill a portion to keep them all from starving."

I had a happy surprise for him. Before I left Shīrāz, the Tribal Office

N.G.S. PHOTOGRAPHER BRUCE DALE (ABOVE); ROLAND MICHAUD

Crossing a rocky plain, family groups and their livestock trudge along as Qashqā'ī have done for three centuries in Fārs Province. In autumn the land along the trail between sharp stone ridges of the Zāgros lies bleak and ungiving. If winter rains fall—many years suffer drought—grass covers the treeless expanse. Each day of migration begins with breaking camp and tying all family goods onto pack animals. One man (holding poles) wears a tribal robe, rarely seen today. Young men enjoy a sprint before starting the daily five-mile march.

ROLAND MICHAUD (ABOVE AND LOWER RIGHT); REZA FAZEL

Dancing at a wedding, girls languidly wave scarfs and glide slowly in a circle to drumbeats and the endless whine of the karnā, *or horn. Relatives feast; bride and groom remain apart until his father brings her to the marriage tent, bids them "Be happy," and leaves them alone. Out-*

side, gifts collect: a dyed, decorated ram; goats; firewood, rare in the treeless plains and much valued.

had asked me to tell Nader that he could leave in three days. Nader hugged me joyously.

"Can't you finish your school work in the next three days and start the move with us?" he asked. "Have you a horse for me?" I asked, for I particularly love the beginning of migration. "*Bali, bali!* Yes, yes! There's always a horse for you!"

I could see the white tent up and ready for business, the children sitting on the bright rugs, waiting quietly like a covey of partridges in the shade. But the Qashqā'ī have a saying: "All drinks should be repeated, and drunk one after the other." This especially applies to tea for the visitor.

The second glass of tea had been swallowed, melting the lump of sugar in my mouth; now I could go to the children.

"Who wants to go to the blackboard?" I asked. Every right arm flew up, every young voice clamored, "*Man! Man!*—Me! Me!" I chose two second-grade boys and gave them a long multiplication problem. "Go!" Chanting each step as loudly and rapidly as auctioneers, they multiplied and added up the figures. The race was a tie and everybody, including the watching fathers, applauded.

I tested every child—in reading, spelling, science, geography, or history. "Tell me about our tribe, the Qashqā'ī," I said to a fourth-grader. He stood poised, without a trace of shyness, and his voice rang out like an orator's, grand and flowing:

"The Qashqā'ī are the most numerous nomadic shepherds of Fārs, numbering about 150,000 people in five large allied tribes, each with tens of subtribes divided into numerous family groups. No one knows our exact origin. But our Turkish dialect and place-names such as Tabrīz in our songs and stories show that we must have lived for a long time in the Caucasus between the Black and Caspian Seas. Some say we first came to Iran in the armies of Genghis Khan and Tamerlane, but we do not accept this. We look at our Aryan features and brown skin and say this cannot be true. We believe we have always lived in Iran and came to Fārs about 300 years ago.

"Some say *Qashqā'ī* means 'horse with a white spot on its forehead,' and that may be right. In the old days, tribes were named after the color of markings of animals and the Qashqā'ī have always believed that a horse with a white forehead brings good luck . . ."

He could have kept on, but I wanted to hear others. They spoke in Persian, which they begin to study in the first grade and learn quickly. Examinations over, I was talking with the fathers and praising Fazel for his good teaching when someone tugged at the hem of my jacket.

A six-year-old girl in long pink tribal dress looked up with demanding eyes. A simple sling held her left arm. "I fell off my donkey on the way. But my right arm is all right and I know a lot and I want to go to the blackboard." I sent her and called out three long words. Singing out each sound, she quickly wrote them all. "Very good!" She raised her chin proudly; she was satisfied. And so was I.

For I suddenly had the same thought about her that I had some years ago about a 10-year-old Fazel: "You'll make a fine teacher one day."

ROLAND MICHAUD

When the new Tribal Teachers School opened in 1956 in Shīrāz, only boys were allowed by their families to come for the year of training. But beginning in 1960, girls have come too, a revolutionary change in tribal life, and one that gives me particular pleasure. What a magnificent and colorful scene with the girls going to class in full tribal dress!

Until 1966, except for the few who won a place in the Teachers School, talented but poor tribal boys and girls had no further chance for education. Then His Majesty's personal interest made possible a six-year boarding high school in Shīrāz, free for the 75 tent-school graduates each year who perform best in competitive tests. A thrill of excitement still runs through me whenever I walk into the low brick building and see these bright-faced, eager young people. I am so proud when they score higher—and they often do—than students in other high schools. And I can hardly wait until its first graduates, the class of 1972, enter the newly built Pahlavi University in Shīrāz, or until they begin work as technicians, agriculturists, engineers, businessmen, and scholars.

While Nader and our cousins prepared for the hard walk south, I visited other tent schools of the Amaleh tribe, and some of the nearby Dareh-Shūrī. On the way from Shīrāz I had stopped to see the Kashkulī-Bozorg around Ardakān, the Shesh-Bolūkī near Ābādeh, and the Fārsī-Madān by the snow-capped peak of Kūh-e Dīnār.

I returned to Nader's tent about midnight before the day he would break camp. In the half-light of dawn, Shahnaz got their two small boys out of their bedding of *jājīm,* or carpet-cloth, on the tent floor, and into Nader's jeep. Crunchy nān in hand to eat on the way, they left with a driver and some women relatives for Nader's house in Shīrāz. Nader's men then loaded into a rented truck everything in the tent from the short-legged 12-foot loom with its unfinished carpet-cloth to the transistor radio and wicker baskets of squawking chickens. I could see that down the slope my cousins Abdollah and Ali were loading too, but on live transport. Donkeys flung open their mouths to let out heaving shrieks as sacks, carpets, and children landed on their backs. Camels sat on folded legs, bellowing and wagging their heads in annoyance that their long summer rest had ended.

"Why do the Qashqā'ī use large numbers of camels and the other tribes of Fārs do not?" I have been asked. Aside from needing them on longer migration routes, the Qashqā'ī regard the camel as a status symbol. "Your family has only donkeys," children taunt each other. A camel, like a Mercedes-Benz, is big, powerful, and expensive, able to bear long tent poles, heavy sacks, and large rugs.

Nader saw the last bundle in place and called for the big tent to come down, a moment that marked the official end of summer camp. Below our knoll, the smaller tents of our cousins began to sink limply one by one. Most families fold their yards and yards of black woven goat hair every morning of the migration and unfold them by noon to make their open-side box tent. In winter camp, the shape is altered: A tall row of center poles gives a pitched roof for shedding rain—we pray there will be rain to shed. Opening the short end (rather than the

Robust toddler fends off growing chill at day's end with sweater and scarfs over tribal dress and tunic. Children in the clan camps now receive vaccinations and instruction in hygiene from public-health officers and tent-school teachers.

KAZEM AHMADI

Badge of the Qashqā'ī, a
kolāh do gūsh — *cap two*
ear — sits saucily on a
small tribesman's curls.
When he grows up, he
probably will not follow
in his father's footsteps
as a shepherd. He may
become a literate worker
in office, factory, or oil
field; a police officer; a
college-trained techni-
cian or professional man.

long side) lets in fresh air, usually mild but occasionally freezing cold.

"Abdollah has our horses," Nader said. "He's always first to move, so we'd better go down and mount. Your driver can go ahead to Chesh-meh-ye Alī, where we'll camp, and wait for us there."

On the nearby hillsides, shepherds ran after flocks, dogs barked and bounded after strays. As the edge of the sun appeared over Āq Dāgh, our White Mountain, camels rose with high-pitched staccato grunts; little girls switched the donkeys, calling "hoish, hoish" to get them started, and the procession of animals and people began to move. I saw Fazel with the school tent on one side of a camel, the blackboard on the other — he hoped to squeeze in a few more hours of teaching.

Nader and I mounted and followed. He rode a fine chestnut stallion, the only pure Arabian he has kept. Such glorious animals, once the pride of the Qashqā'ī Khāns, are fast disappearing. Expensive to keep and breed, they are much less useful than a jeep. One man I know actually gave his Arabian for a jeep on even trade!

Most horses of the Qashqā'ī are like the one I rode, smaller unpedi-greed animals, still handsome and intelligent, fast and reliable, but not as magnificent as the great Arabians of the past. Exhibition riding is fading out too. At weddings sometimes, my cousin Mansur and a few others will still gallop their horses and lean out of the saddle to pick up a handkerchief, or jump from saddle to ground and back, time after time as the horses run. But I've heard of no young person practicing such fancy riding skills.

Of course, most Qashqā'ī men can shoot well from a galloping horse — even I can do it — and Nader has been a prize-winning shot and horseman for two decades. As we started on the track for Cheshmeh-ye Alī, Nader said, "Right over there is the place where I shot a dozen wild boar some days ago," and pointed toward Āq Dāgh. "I was sitting in my tent when Ali ran up out of breath to tell me a large pack was moving across our plain to Qara Dāgh. I grabbed my rifle and jumped on my horse, taking no time to saddle. I saw 12 boars running together, grunting and squealing, long tusks flashing. I galloped past them, first on one side, then on the other, shooting as I went. I managed to kill every one." It would have surprised me if he had not. No Moslem should eat pork — no hunter would refuse such fine sport.

We arrived at the pass called Galavar ahead of the procession. I could see Nader's clan coming toward us along a shallow ravine. One group, then another a quarter-mile back, then another, and still another came riding and walking over a low rise, about 15 groups in all. By each one, men walked with sheep and goats that hastily nibbled at almost invisibly small bits of dry stubble and thistle leaves.

Just then, along a path running at the base of the large hill opposite us, I saw another procession: our friend Habib's clan. Habib galloped his horse to us, and he and Nader decided that Nader's people would go first through the pass and take the track on the left side of the valley. Habib's families would follow and take the right. Shepherds like such an arrangement; it minimizes crowding with its dangers of accidents and injuries, and flocks don't get mixed. Both clans would camp at Cheshmeh-ye Alī—Ali's Spring—so friends could visit each other.

In the old days, before the 1950's, the Khāns sometimes chose to put on a show of strength and would instruct the lower chiefs to bring all their people and animals to one place. I have seen 5,000 families trying to crowd through a pass, or cross a river at one ford. Dust would rise like smoke from a great fire when they spread out across a plain— 25,000 people with perhaps a half million sheep and goats, 20,000 horses, 50,000 donkeys, and 5,000 to 10,000 dogs. A vast army, dramatic, frightening—and nerve-racking for the animals' owners.

As Nader's families passed by us into the defile, everyone nodded and smiled to me, but faces quickly resumed an anxious solemnity: With the drought, grass to the south would become more scant each day, dust worse, heat more oppressive. Even the young girls, usually spirited and singing ''Run, run, run away, my dear'' to the donkeys, walked in silence. I could hear hundreds of little hoofs strike the rocky ground, a sound like the rhythmic patter of light rain on a tile roof.

Nader and I lingered behind talking, following no track, hoping to flush a covey of partridges. Not a one fluttered up. Drought afflicts them too. About 11 o'clock when we arrived at Cheshmeh-ye Alī, the goods from the camels' and donkeys' loads already sat in piles on the ground. Men inserted slotted poles into the corner loops of black cloth and deftly raised each tent roof. Mallet sounds bumped each other unevenly as women and children helped pound stakes into the stony earth. Tent sides were fastened to the roof with wooden pins, open front facing away from the east-west arc of the hot sun. Sacks and bundles were stacked into a row under each tent, rugs shaken and spread. Fires began heating up teapots while pack animals and horses were watered and feedsacks tied over their muzzles. Off toward the horizon, the flocks grazed.

Just as Nader and I settled down to tea in Abdollah's tent, Ali ran up and said in some excitement, ''Habib wants me to drive the jeep to Semirom and bring back the midwife for one of the women in his clan.'' In a moment he was roaring off. I mentioned to the men gathered around the campfire that only two years earlier there would have been no midwife to fetch. Instead, the husband would have been shooting a gun into the air, hoping to scare away evil spirits said to kill women in childbirth by eating their livers. Now the Qashqā'ī have 12 midwives, and as many more will be trained each year in a new program sponsored by Empress Farah. Their skill and knowledge will help keep tribal mothers and babies alive.

I had to return to Shīrāz as soon as Ali arrived with the midwife, for hundreds of applicants for midwife school, high school, teachers' school, and teachers' jobs would arrive in a few days to take examinations. For months after that fall migration, drought continued to oppress the nomads of Iran. But I have learned that the baby delivered that day at Cheshmeh-ye Alī was a boy—the first for a man with three daughters. Shots were fired into the air with happy shouts; the *karnā*, or horn, whined its tune; girls danced with scarfs and boys fought mock battles with sticks, to welcome this addition to a new generation of Qashqā'ī.

Sipping hot tea starts the shepherd's day, punctuates it several times, and

ROLAND MICHAUD (BELOW AND LOWER RIGHT); ERNEST THOMAS GREENE

ends it. Men brew the drink and often prepare kebab, or meat roasted on skewers. With the keen hunger that hard work brings, tribesmen settle down to the staple dish of rice with bits of meat, cooked by women.

In a friendly joust, veiled Tuareg noblemen of west-central Niger brandish spears and two-edged swords in the

Men of the Veil, Women of Ancien
TUAREG of the Sahara Keep the Styl

By Victor Englebert
Illustrations by the Author

ge-old manner of combat. Warriors and caravaneers and pastoralists, the nomadic Tuareg once ruled the Sahara.

Pride,

of Lords

ALGERIA LIBYA

Ahaggar
Tamanrasset •

Aïr •Bilma
•Agadez
MALI NIGER

A F R I C A

JULY. An implacable sun. An immeasurable land. No horizon. We are walking in the void. Not a landmark to measure our progress. Not a stone, not a blade of grass. Only the sand—white, smooth, and blinding. Soon the wind will sweep away our tracks and the land will look as virgin as ever. Our small caravan stretches silently, mechanically, as insignificant in this ocean of fire as the grains of sand it treads. Miles—abstract like the hours.

All the camels have the same air of assurance and disdain. It is said that they alone know the hundredth name of Allāh. My two companions, veiled to the eyes as the custom of their society requires, seem without expression.

Amud and Litni are Tuareg of the Central Sahara—Berber nomads. For centuries this desolate magnificence has divided the Mediterranean world from the lesser-known lands of Africa, but the caravans of cameleers like these have sustained commerce between them. I met my companions at the market of Tamanrasset, the last Algerian village on the road from Alger to Agadez, an important stop in the midst of nowhere. Amud I knew: I had spent a few days in his camp five years before. I remembered some words of Tamahaq, his language, and he speaks a little French.

In this journey we follow Tuareg ways—as clear to these people, and as complex to outsiders, as star patterns and dune shapes that guide us in a land of no roads. Amud and Litni are *Ihaggaren*, members of the federation of the Ahaggar Mountains in Algeria, Tuareg famed all over the Sahara for the endurance of their camels. They keep this identity even though insufficient pastures drove their families south a few decades ago to the Talak, a region of sparse grass and scrub in the west-central portion of the Republic of Niger. They are keeping their Algerian nationality as well.

Amud and Litni came to Tamanrasset to sell camels and had disposed of all but three. They hoped to find buyers for these in the Aïr Mountains, although this route would lengthen the journey home to camp. I asked permission to ride with them, quickly adding that I had experience with camels. For long seconds, Amud stared at me through the slit of his veil, but if he was surprised he did not say so. Then he turned and, in a wide and noble gesture that revealed the fullness of his long indigo robe, indicated a beautiful white camel. "It is yours for as long as you wish to stay with us," he said.

We traveled through black volcanic mountains for several days. Now we amble across an arm of the great *ténéré*—uninhabited desert— that spreads like a sea of sand around the Ahaggar and the Aïr. From it both massifs rise like islands. At times alluring mirages re-establish the horizon. Images of fresh pools dance in my mind, but I ignore them. For one cannot have everything. Here is peace, silence, purity.

On this march we are walking full south. In early day we project immense shadows on our right. They shorten progressively, disappear

A chieftain of the noble Iullimiden tribe, Mohammed swathes his face and head with the traditional tagilmust. *Men over the age of 15 or 16 wear these 20-foot scarfs, concealing all but their eyes before strangers of their own society. With outsiders they may disregard the customs that govern adjustment of the veil. Mohammed's camp reflects the complexity of Tuareg groups, with some eighty families of nobles, vassals, craftsmen, and servants.*

Belgian-born photojournalist VICTOR ENGLEBERT, *who now lives in New York City, has traveled extensively in Africa, Asia, and Latin America.*

East of the Aïr Mountains, a caravan of 100 camels (below) transports salt hundreds of miles from beds at Bilma oasis to markets in southern Niger. Tuareg traders make this arduous journey every year to barter salt for food, cloth, and household utensils. In the salt-gathering process (right), a workman pours water into potholes to loosen the crystals. At left, caravaneers remain on the march while eating a gruel of millet, water, and dried goat cheese.

Pulling grass ropes, girls haul a leather bucket of fresh water from a 20-foot-deep well in the Talak area, where rains in summer support sparse grass. The girl at left has the rank of a vassal; her companion, of a servant. Above, a vassal closes the neck of a goatskin water bag with a straw cord before hanging it up to season. She has filled it with the reddish-brown solution of acacia bark that waterproofs the hide.

under the bellies of our camels and reappear on our left, lengthening now. We shall not eat before night, for there is no shade to prepare a meal in and above all nothing for the camels to nibble. A Tuareg does not stop to eat when his camels fast.

A hot wind keeps the sand suspended in the air, joining the earth to the sky without a seam. It rushes into my companions' robes, spreading them wide, giving them all manner of weird shapes. The veils give more remoteness to my faceless friends.

I too am veiled to the eyes. I know, having lost skin to the sun, the uses of the long *tagilmust*, the Tuareg turban-veil. Its cover helps prevent the mouth from drying; like sunglasses it tones down the glare of the sand. No doubt Tuareg men began veiling themselves on long marches in the desert; in these women took no part, and to this day they have not adopted veils. Ages went by, I suppose, and the veil became supremely important to the modest man. Elaborate custom governs the adjustments of the tagilmust. No well-bred Tuareg would remove it before women, old people, or strangers within his own society, least of all before his wife's parents. To eat and drink he will often pass his glass or spoon under it.

The sun has reached the end of its course. In half an hour, nothing will remain of its wrath but a little blood in the sky, which night will drink. It is the serene hour. Amud and Litni, as good Moslems, prostrate themselves to the east for the fourth prayer.

We go on, late into the night. When we stop, Litni hobbles the camels, leads them into a circle, and dumps a bundle of grass in their midst. He lights a fire and prepares tea and *taguila*, a flat whole-grain wheat bread baked in the ashes. Wood as well as food and fodder are carried by the camels in these empty wastes.

Amud, lying on his back, sings at the top of his voice. Chores are not for him. He is an *amahar*; he belongs to the noble Kel Rela tribe. Amahar (*imaheren*, in the plural) may designate any person of Tuareg culture and language—and the name Tuareg, which is Arab, is not used. But in its strict sense amahar means "one in full possession of freedom and political rights, one who is noble." Amud is a noble and Litni his *amrid*, or vassal.

To almost any generalization Tuareg society offers exceptions; but usually a noble tribe could claim dues of millet from its vassals, with livestock and butter in times of good grazing. It might claim—and even secure—service in war against other tribes, as in European feudalism. But ideas of hierarchy, of higher and lower classes, do not fit Tuareg thought. Tamahaq has no words for comparative or superlative degree. One can only say a person belongs to this group or to that, and the Tuareg recognize many social groupings. The *inislimen* are religious tribes, scrupulous in Islam. *Enaden* are smiths and craftsmen. *Imrad*—vassals—of mixed Arab-Tuareg descent have special rank.

Iklan—the so-called slaves—are born into the role of servants, but their position follows patterns of kinship. They could not be sold. If one chose to, he could change "masters," and the first "owner" would lose much prestige. Today some iklan are starting herds of their own;

many seek a new life as laborers in uranium mines, oil fields, and towns.

Now the taguila is cooked. Litni pulls it out of the embers, scrapes its crust free of ashes with his nails, washes it in a little water, breaks it into pieces in a copper basin. I add the contents of three sardine tins, and we eat. Later, stretched out on the soft sand, I gaze at the most beautiful sky in the world, a perfect dome luminous with stars. A few paces away, the dying fire casts intermittent glimmers. . . .

It is crackling again when I awake at dawn.

Amud and Litni sit near it, watching the kettle. They rose long before first light, to say the first prayer, and a new taguila has been cooked. When the sun rises we are already in the saddle.

On entering the Aïr Mountains, we go single file on rocky tracks, side by side in sandy valleys—sometimes nonstop for 16 hours. Two or three times we find a Tuareg encampment and spend the night there. Then Litni, like Amud, takes the role of a guest; closely veiled, he sits dignified on a straw mat to accept due hospitality.

I can tell when we are approaching a camp. Amud and Litni put on the new robes they wore in Tamanrasset; they rewind the tagilmust with care. To conform with custom, we always stop our camels 40 or 50 paces from the tents and wait for someone to greet us.

This afternoon we reach a large encampment, at least eight tents visible among the scrub. Men help us unload our camels, and we sit in comfort on straw mats. A boy goes for tea and sugar while other men join us, among them the chief, called Biga.

While Litni exchanges news with them, I watch our hosts closely. Their profiles are less aquiline than Amud's. Their limbs are short and powerful, their hands square and strong. "They are imrad of an Iforas tribe," Amud tells me, "originally from the Adrar Mountains in Mali. They fled that massif a few decades ago—their imaheren were becoming too greedy." Such action has long been a pattern among the Tuareg, and helps explain the dispersal of various tribesmen.

Nomadic Tuareg wander over an area roughly defined by Reggane in Algeria, Ghudāmis in Libya, Tombouctou in Mali, and Zinder in Niger. Traditionally, tribesmen remained within territories defined by the leaders of their federation. The federation—there are five of these —would assign grazing rights to its members, to assure that they would remain peacefully apart most of the year and would gather at a set place and time for a pleasant reunion. Even today many Tuareg respect these boundaries—national borders mean less to them. The most important distinction of all is that between the rigorous country of the Sahara proper and the more hospitable savanna south of it.

Men of the Iforas come from neighboring encampments to Biga's and everyone tries the camels my companions offer for sale. In a trade with the Tuareg an outsider must take his chances; among themselves bargaining follows well-understood ritual. At last the animals are exchanged for money, the best of the three for the equivalent of $200.

Livestock, I learn, sells for a good profit in Libya, where oil revenues increase wealth, and some of the Iforas are planning a long journey to sell sheep there. I have never traveled in the Sahara with flocks; I tell

Biga of my interest in this. "You are welcome to join us," he says. "We shall leave on the 27th day of the tenth Moslem month. Be here a day before." I promise that he can expect me that day.

Setting out the next morning for the Talak, we walk several days more. One morning, seeing Amud and Litni putting on their newest robes, I know that our journey will end today.

Amud's brother Bukush comes out to welcome us when we reach a group of three tents. We enter the largest. An old woman sits in a corner — Amud's mother. As he addresses her respectfully, Litni explains to me that she is a widow. Only after ten minutes does Amud take leave to go and greet his wife. Not that he does not love her — far from that — but a Tuareg pays respects to his parents first.

Returning with his young wife Fati and a baby daughter called Shina, Amud takes off two-thirds of his long tagilmust and winds it back more loosely, in a less formal fashion. He is home again.

AMUD, Fati, and Shina share one tent; his brother Talem, Sata, their three daughters and little son, another. The mother's tent also houses Bukush, who is a widower, his daughter Ataka, age 9, and an unmarried sister called Maunen. I refuse vehemently when they insist on giving up Amud's tent to me. They move it 20 paces — to a suitable distance for a visitor. I argue that I prefer to sleep under the stars, but to no avail. I come to feel somewhat better, however, when I realize that this tent helps me to be a good host. Visitors call frequently, and I can serve tea "in my own house."

In long conversations I explain that there are no camels in France, that a Frenchman pays no bride-price. I learn that an amahar must pay his parents-in-law four she-camels for his bride, besides feeding wedding guests. As for property or money, the Tuareg think in terms of usefulness — money is useful to buy useful things.

Wedding arrangements are complicated. The Tuareg man, who is monogamous, thinks it best to marry his mother's brother's daughter. His father's sister's daughter is also a proper bride. Such cousins always enjoy a special joking relationship; they become good friends, and can expect a stable marriage. Women are held in great respect; they speak their opinions freely. A wife may chat with a former suitor, and society would reprove the husband if he showed any jealousy.

And the Tuareg love children, any children. The youngsters themselves are adorable: respectful, easy to handle — though if a parent gets a little too severe, which is rare, the child will spit or throw sand and not run away from blows. Then somebody else usually takes the child up to soothe it, and the trouble disappears. Children often go naked till the age of 4 or 5, unless dressed for protection on desert marches.

It is touching to observe Ataka's love for her father. She helps him in everything, even to saddling his camel — normally a boy's chore. When he is sitting or lying in the tent, she leans against him. Bukush tells me that after he lost his wife, he nursed Ataka from babyhood, even carrying her in his arms on camelback.

Abela, Talem's little son, is the only boy in the family. He is strong and fearless, ready to grab anything he can reach, including insects of the most repulsive kind. When he frightens the older girls with them, his father and uncles look on with pride. "A real amahar," they say with a smile of satisfaction. Though he is too young for clothes, they let him wear a man's dagger at his waist and play with it freely.

Sometimes at noon the wind rises and blows sand. The Tuareg close the "tent wall," the *asaber*, a thick straw mat artistically interwoven with leather strips. We cover our heads and doze for a couple of hours, for the days begin early.

With their mournful and monotonous moans, the 16 or 17 young camels tethered near the tents wake everybody up long before dawn. Bujimra, the young servant, brings the dams to them. A teapot sings on a bed of embers before every tent; women and children sit around, still only half-awake. Usually the three brothers are off in the pastures watching their camels, for all their iklan except Bujimra have left.

A man may help himself to a camel he needs, provided he notifies someone, without being a thief; but outside his own federation he considers all rules are off. And Tuareg who used to think plunder the noblest of activities find it hard to live by other ideals. Imaheren take camels by force—or at least they used to.

An amahar does not herd sheep or goats. Therefore Amud and his brothers keep no flocks. If they did, the family would take the animals to the well daily to water them; as it is, the women make this trip, some three or four miles, about every five days. They can bring water enough for two or three days, and when the supply is used up we fall back on camel's milk. With a little millet, milk is the staple food.

Only a few years ago Amud's family had gardens in the Ahaggar, cultivated by Harratin, people who worked as sharecroppers. These yielded tomatoes and figs, and enough wheat to barter some for dates from the oasis of Tidikelt. But the Harratin have taken work elsewhere. Times change, though days keep a familiar rhythm.

In the evening, sometimes, a drum sounds: invitation to an *ahal*, a gathering of the young. I wind my tagilmust closely, saddle my camel, and follow the sound in the moonless night. I find young women seated on the ground, beating the drum, clapping their hands, and singing songs of elaborate rhyme schemes and subtle rhythms. Closely veiled men, armed with spears and swords and mounted high on elegant camels, make their animals dance around the girls, the gaits changing in patterns to fit the cadence of the songs.

Tonight I sit near the women while the immense silhouettes turn around us high on the sky and the whole beautiful starry dome seems to turn with them. A woman improvises praise of men she likes: their clothes are dark as the night, their camels white as the moon . . . through the blue tagilmust, as long as six spears, shine eyes of embers . . . they come to torture the heart . . . . In fact they come to pay tribute to the girls, for beautiful they are. Tuareg women often have the strange and wild beauty—unexpected and ravishing—of flowers growing in hostile places. *(Continued on page 127)*

In the camp of the author's friend Amud, his sister-in-law Sata dyes a small goatskin; his mother waits for her eldest granddaughter to serve tea. During the day, noblewomen often gather to chat and make household items. At right, a mother tends her children while painting a leather pouch. An upturned bowl makes a drum for a girl who chants as her companions clap to the rhythm.

Versed in the Koran, a marabout, or holy man, with dip pen and wooden
slate teaches scripture to an attentive boy. Smudged from play, a girl too
young for lessons rests on the lap of her cousin. With her big toe and her
small friend helping to control the tautness of her yarn, a girl spins dyed
wool on a light distaff. Overleaf: Reclining on a red carpet, Bukush and
Ataka, his motherless 9-year-old daughter, escape the midday heat.

Shaking a whip of twisted rawhide (above), 2½-year-old Abela chases young camels near the tents. Below left, he encourages a 6-week-old calf to join the others. Playing now, Abela will handle large herds by the age of 9. Maunen drags an obstinate calf from its mother after it has nursed.

Amud's family now herds only camels; other Tuareg raise sheep, goats, and cattle as well.

But I must leave this harsh country, this fascinating life, to see something of the southern Tuareg, by far the most numerous, who live in savanna areas. With richer and wider pastures, they own larger herds, including many cattle. Their life differs accordingly. I can journey as far as Agadez with an amrid from a neighboring camp; he has business there, and will lend me a camel.

While I pack, my friends seem unusually quiet. The women and children sit at a distance; Amud helps me load my camel. It would be so easy to remain with them forever. I distribute little presents to everyone without saying goodbye. The Tuareg do not speak of the end of a sojourn but of the beginning of a journey; their words at partings are devout words for an enterprise begun: *Bismallāh* — In the Name of God. *Inshallāh* — As God Wills.

Amud walks with us for half a mile. Then — Bismallāh! — we mount our camels and leave him without looking back.

In Agadez I rent a Land-Rover and hire an interpreter who can introduce me to the people I want to meet, Iullimiden nobles who wander in the Azaouak region of Niger.

If custom is prized among the Tuareg, so is adaptability. For some eight centuries tribespeople have settled in villages and towns, as some are settling today. My interpreter is a sedentary Tuareg; a turbanless man whose father — in the French army for years — named him Carbochi after a Corsican adjutant. Brought up in Agadez, Carbochi learned French there although he never went to school.

Scattered trees and patches of grass had begun to change the face of the desert on the way south to Agadez. Farther south, I notice green leaves more and more often. We are leaving the Sahara definitely behind, entering savanna country. Without difficulty one afternoon we reach the encampment of the Iullimiden, guided from the well of Tchin Tabaraden by a smith of theirs whom we met at the market. The whole savanna is dotted with tents, but the smith takes us to the largest, the chief's. Some 30 by 50 feet, this is the biggest tent I have yet seen.

Mohammed, the chief, a man about 45, and his wife Fatimatu receive us cordially. Yet hardly are the greetings over than Carbochi starts ridiculing the figures of Fatimatu and her daughter-in-law Raishatu. "You are as big as a Berliet" — a huge French truck. True, they are enormous, but I urge him to shut up.

"I am an amrid," he explains to me. "None of my words could soil a noblewoman. If I were an amahar, Mohammed might already have killed me. In her youth many men died for Fatimatu's sake." And indeed the ladies show nothing but amusement at his words.

Perhaps his remarks passed as compliments, for noblemen want their women as fat as possible. In Amud's family women were slim because they had to work. But the Iullimiden still have many iklan, great herds of camels and of cattle, and their women can loll about all day. From the age of 8 or 9 girls are gorged with milk and by the age of 12 they already look adult. The fatter a woman, the richer her husband appears, the greater his prestige. The men remain lean, trim enough to handle the swords that made their supremacy.

Tuareg maiden evokes deeds of tribal heroes with an anzad, *an instrument rather like a violin. A taut bow drawn across one horsehair string yields sounds that resonate in the leather-covered calabash. "Skilled women produce beautiful, haunting music," says the author, "and often accompany it with improvised poems of their own."*

Fatimatu, who sits in her tent like a queen, is very proud of that superiority. "Even the French," she says, "would not have beaten us without their firearms. Before they came we were invulnerable, as powerful as de Gaulle. We, the Iullimiden, ruled and plundered from Tombouctou to Lake Chad. Everything bent before us. We took slaves and anything we wanted. When an amrid died, we inherited all his possessions." Decimated by endless wars and uneducated by the standards of today, the Iullimiden have retained relatively little of their ancient power but they are still people to be reckoned with.

While we converse with Mohammed and Fatimatu, their son Radwane—Raishatu's husband—orders one of his father's men to place our luggage in his own tent. This, though half the size of his father's, is large compared to those of the vassals.

A sheep is slaughtered in my honor and, to my surprise, I am also served macaroni. But this family is very rich, Carbochi tells me, and often eats macaroni or rice and couscous. They eat gazelle or bustard, too, for the men spend some of their leisure hunting. All these imaheren have rifles and pistols in their tents.

After our lavish meal a noblewoman gives a recital on the *anzad,* or one-stringed violin. In our midst sits the musician, amazingly expert at pulling varied sounds from that simple instrument, with two men singing. The airs, with a 12-tone scale and leaps of melody, would swiftly break European voices. We clap hands to the beat. Moving and lovely, the songs escape one by one to the stars.

Next morning I try to count the tents, but they are scattered in every direction. Mohammed himself is not sure how many there are: "Maybe 70 or 80," he says. What a fine sight it must be when all these people are moving together! But I will not have a chance to see it. With iklan to tend the herds it does not matter how far the pastures are, and the tents may stay as long as four months at the same site. Amud, by contrast, sometimes left a site after only a week, and two months was a very long stay for him.

Mohammed can say that only 8 of these tents belong to imaheren, all close relatives of his. The rest belong to his satellites. The enaden alone occupy 13 tents, so rich are the Iullimiden to support such an army of artisans. The men forge spears, swords, and knives, or silver jewels; they make camel saddles and wooden beds, carve wooden bowls and spoons. The women weave beautiful tent-wall mats or produce artistic leatherwork—wallets, amulets, bags, cushions.

Other Tuareg hold blacksmiths in wary respect because of their mysterious connivance with fire, their dangerous mystic power called *ettama,* and their sharp wits, quick to compose a song of ridicule.

Although little action seems to take place, life here is not at all monotonous. People visit from group to group. I spend most of the time among the women, for it is they, teachers of the children, who also teach language and custom to the stranger accepted as worthy of learning. The language here differs from that of the north, slightly in vocabulary and considerably in pronunciation.

Often we write and decipher Tifinagh, an ancient Libyan script which most Tuareg know. It has only one symbol for all vowel sounds and can be written left-to-right-right-to-left or up-down-up-down, which does not simplify it for beginners.

All too quickly the days slip by. I have made friends it hurts to leave, but far to the north Biga and his people will be setting out on their long journey, the caravan of dune and mountain and plain, on the march as in time immemorial. Promising to return with the help of God—Inshallāh—I climb into the Land-Rover with Carbochi and we speed to the mountains of Aïr.

On the appointed day we reach the Iforas' encampment. Biga declares I am a man of my word. Now I notice the tents with more interest: little things of canvas or leather, hardly five feet square. Even the iklan have larger tents in the Azaouak. Although Iforas tents are unimpressive and clothes almost ragged, the herds are large. Considering the trade these people carry north and south, they must be much less poor than they look.

At any rate, the men are all quite well dressed next morning for the departure. Today is an exceptionally auspicious day to begin a journey and Biga's people are preparing three different caravans.

Those going to Libya have the hardest and longest march, more than 600 miles one way, three months at least for the trip. A second group will go to the Amadror valley about 500 miles north to mine salt. Theirs will be a 40-day trip. Later, they will barter salt for millet, south in the Damergou region. The third group is going south to Zinder, about 500 miles away, to buy millet—another 40-day trek.

Around 9:30 a.m. the camels are brought to the tents and loaded. Helped by some women and children, two men gather the sheep and goats. All is done without haste, shouts, or flurry.

This work finished, the men sit down around two marabouts, or holy men, who read aloud from a pocket Koran and blow in turn on the muddy water in a small enamel teapot. The water thus blessed, the pot is passed around and each traveler drinks from it. This protects them from getting lost, losing animals, or dying of thirst.

Now one of the marabouts sacrifices a kid and all the men, standing, say a prayer. The marabout shakes every man's hand and our caravan gets slowly under way for Libya while he chants: "Lā Ilāh Illā Allāh; Muḥammad rasūl Allāh—There is no God but God; Mohammed is the Prophet of God."

Women standing nearby watch the men disappear, none glancing behind him. I follow on camelback. Guided by a man of the Iforas, Carbochi will take the Land-Rover ahead and meet us every night.

Three men drive the flock before them: some thirty goats and ten times as many sheep. Half a dozen men follow on camels, each leading four camels or more. Before crossing the great plain of desert sand they will spend two days cutting wood and grass. Each will load one camel with wood, two with fodder, one or two with water.

Biga, riding at my side, says he will turn back after a few days. "I am only along to help at the start and to show the men my concern," he says. He explains that they will stop for a couple of days at Djanet, in

Algeria, and sell any animals too weak to go on. It will take a month to reach Ghāt, in Libya. There stock brings ten times the price in Agadez: $50 per sheep, say, instead of $5. Even the few donkeys trotting along, despicable animals worth a dollar or two in Niger, will fetch $15 or $30 at Ghāt. The men will remain a few weeks in Ghāt to make purchases and let the camels rest. They will return with clothes and fabric, wheat, dates, sugar, tea, and other goods, part to be sold in neighboring encampments.

Late in the day we reach a place appointed for meeting caravaneers from other camps. We unload the camels. The men who have driven the flock sink down to rest and two others take the animals to pasture for the night. Each man has a precise job, the same for the whole journey. The three youngest pound millet every morning and evening, and are responsible for wood and water. The three next in age drive the flock. Two others take the animals to graze after each day's march. The rest will take care of the camels.

While we sit around the fire that evening a man walks into the edge of the circle of light. Some of my companions had lowered their veils somewhat; quickly each raises the tagilmust again to his eyes, and then the man comes forward. We see he is a stranger. Politely he exchanges greetings with us. Finally he says that his water bag is empty and he has been thirsty for a very long time. A bowlful of water is poured and he gulps it down after pronouncing the ritual praise to God.

"Since sunset," he says, "I have been following sounds of pestles hitting mortars and of children crying, but every time I thought I was going to find an encampment, the sound stopped suddenly—only to start somewhere else."

"*Kel Asuf—Djinnen*," my friends murmur, and the man nods.

The Tuareg credit tales of djinns, or spirits. They always have extravagant stories of demons. I am incredulous—but not in the least skeptical of the dangers our guest had faced while he was lost.

Again at sunrise the sheep and goats are led away. We make our way through the mountains, passing heaps of basalt that rise like pyramids. We thread narrow canyons or broad wadis overhung with trees. We pass dozens of gazelles. They observe us with wonder, then spring into a graceful gallop. When they are not too far away, Biga dismounts with his rifle and stalks them from behind his camel. Once he aims, a gazelle can be counted dead. These men need meat, and cannot afford to kill many of their flock.

We reach the arm of the grand ténéré that I crossed with Amud and Litni many weeks ago. Now my civilization claims me again. Carbochi and I accompany our friends on foot for half a mile; we exchange the ritual Bismallāh. The men of the caravan go on alone and I watch them shrink in the distance with a pinch of the heart.

I wonder how many years are left to the caravans, to the herds of the desert, to the nomads' life. But Carbochi, impatient to get back to town, is pulling at my sleeve; and besides, did Biga ever really exist? Already the wind has blown away his tracks and those of his companions, and like ghosts they are walking in the void, far away, toward no horizon.

Silt-laden pool of rainwater in the jumbled Aïr range provides one of the few waterings for a goat and sheep caravan bound for markets in Libya. Men of a vassal tribe of the Iforas drive the flock of 350 animals across scrub-strewn country during the three-month trip. After selling their stock, the herders will buy clothes, wheat, dates, tea, and sugar, then begin the 600-mile walk home to camp in the mountains.

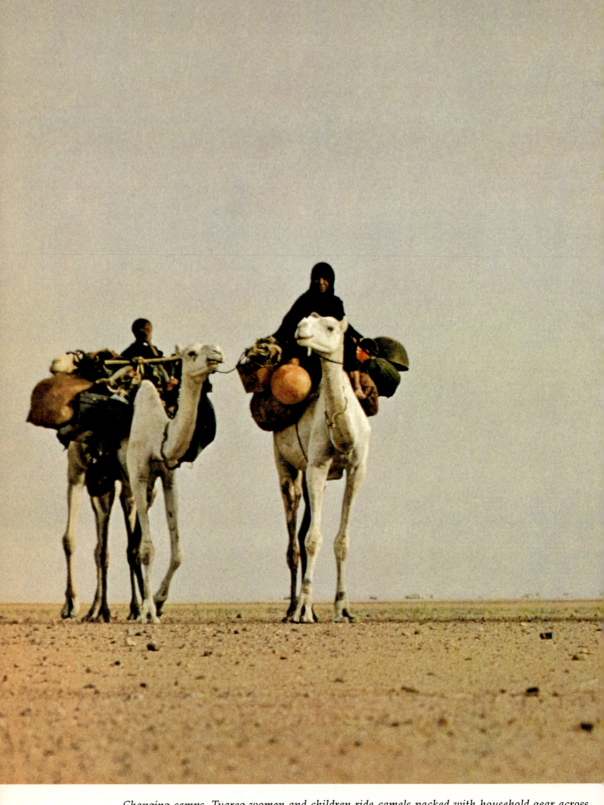

Changing camps, Tuareg women and children ride camels packed with household gear across
a featureless plain. In noble tribes women ride camels only; vassal women often ride donkeys
—or, in savanna country, oxen, also used to transport tents and domestic utensils. For all

*Tuareg wanderers, however, considerations of forage and water hold sovereign importance;
and families cross national boundaries at will. While politics and modernization affect
others in the Sahara, many Tuareg still choose to follow the harsh life of the desert nomad.*

Agile bodies, drumbeats, and quivering leaves thrust into belts stress the music that celebrates a marriage. The m

Forest Peace and Bounty Sustain
BAMBUTI, Pygmy Bands of the Ituri

By Alyette de Munck
Illustrations by the Author

...d women of two Pygmy bands join here as they would to honor any notable event—with dance and song.

Africa's

Ituri R.

Congo R.

Mount Hoyo

UGANDA

Lake Victoria

DEMOCRATIC REPUBLIC OF THE CONGO

Lake Kivu

RWANDA

A F R I C A

AFTER AN ABSENCE of ten years I find myself again in the Ituri Forest, in the heart of Africa. The ice-covered Ruwenzori—Mountains of the Moon—are not far off, the Equator little farther. Yesterday I left my home in Gisenyi, a Rwandan town on Lake Kivu, which is bordered by volcanoes, some still active. I have always lived there; my parents came from Belgium in 1928, to plant coffee.

To reach the Ituri I crossed savannas where antelopes, lions, and elephants wander, then the cold mountain bamboo forests where shaggy gorillas live. Now I drive along a slender corridor of red earth that cuts through the huge and massive rain forest. Enormous trees struggle to keep their heads in the sun, for few things flourish in the damp shade below. Tortured lianas climb grappled to the trees. Great tributaries glide toward the Congo River, fed by many streams. This world draws and absorbs me, and I have always sought occasion to visit its inhabitants the Pygmies, so engaging and so happy.

This time I intend to revisit the group called Efe, of the Bambuti. Even in the name of these small people one finds an enigma, for whatever tongue they originally spoke, they have adopted the languages of their neighbors, the three great Bantu tribes of the Ituri region: the Balese, the Babira, and the Bambuba. In these languages the prefix *Ba* means "people"; *Mu*, "one person." Thus one Pygmy calls himself an Mbuti, his people the Bambuti. The Efe Pygmies live in the forest near Mount Hoyo in the eastern Congo. I do not know how many there are—who can say?—but I know that part of the Ituri well, for I used to go there often before the Democratic Republic of the Congo won a troubled independence in 1960.

I struggle to reach Mount Hoyo. The road is frightful—mud gives way to holes; it takes 17 hours to go 60 miles in the somber forest.

Strangers and the Bantu villagers find that the unknown forest makes them uneasy. For the Pygmies, the Bambuti of the Ituri, it is a refuge where they find protection, food and clothing, healing—all they need for survival. One senses a profound difference between these nomadic hunters and the Bantu farmers, in custom as in size. The Pygmies are much smaller; an Mbuti mother holding her baby has the height of a Mulese girl 7 or 8 years old, just over four feet. They seem in perfect harmony with their forest environment. Has it always sheltered them? The Balese Bantu in this part of the Ituri freely admit the Bambuti were there long before they themselves arrived and that the forest—virgin and intact—is the Pygmies' domain.

At Mount Hoyo the Bambuti welcome me. Among the first to come running to my Volkswagen bus is Hisa, the "chief." Nothing in particular distinguishes him from the others; his authority is relative; he talks a lot, no one listens. He wears a loincloth of fig-tree bark, as do most of the Bambuti. As always, they carry bows and arrows. They seem greatly pleased to see me, and I am pleased to see them.

With sunset I am plunged into the enchantment of the forest. Near

Undohubo, a noted hunter of Bahana's band, takes careful aim. Craftsman as well as archer, he fashioned his wooden bow and its 28-inch, rattan-fiber string. He can temper a hardwood arrow with fire, but this metal arrowhead comes from a Bantu village. The Pygmy bow has a range of about 40 yards. Undohubo missed this shot—at a long-tailed monkey—but with typical Bambuti good nature he expects better luck next time.

Resident in Africa for 43 years, Mme ALYETTE DE MUNCK—who collects poisonous snakes for science—first met the Efe Pygmies in 1952.

Bambuti men raise hoop-framed fishnets from a muddy tributary of the Ituri River only to find them empty. They drag the nets behind them and, even in the low water of the dry season, cannot see a catch until they lift them. The band adopted this method of fishing from Bantu villagers, who make the nets. Women usually wrap fresh fish in leaves to cook them on hot charcoal, sometimes roast them directly on the coals. Below, women and older girls of Bahana's group search for crabs in the Isehe, a smaller, limpid stream that flows from Mount Hoyo. Its water runs so cool between the high, ferny banks that the workers will warm themselves later at a fire. The great rain forest never grows truly hot—about 70° F. at night and barely 80° in the daytime—so Bambuti archers rarely go to the rivers to cool off or, for that matter, take a complete bath.

Brooding over their river-side fire, the women warm themselves after the crab hunt, children sharing their rest. Above, three little boys intently watch one of innumerable Pygmy dances. The tallest, Asumani's son, stands 3 feet, 3 inches at about 11 years and will grow to about 4½ feet at maturity. The smaller are Hisa's, aged approximately 7 and 5. They suck on fresh twigs as they gaze.

me, crickets and frogs give a concert. So from a distance do the Bambuti —one cannot confuse their music with that of the Balese. I recognize the acid and strident sound of bamboo flutes and the heavy rhythm of drums . . . these accompanied by wild and raucous songs.

I plan to spend some time with Hisa and his band: 10 men, 8 women, 16 children. Once there were more, but one, Bahana, went off taking with him some 20 persons, all belonging to his family. A little deeper in the forest is a third group, also part of Hisa's clan, led by Citonu, a man of about 20. A clan includes several groups, the members coming and going as they like; each group is composed of 20 or 30 persons, or more, enough to support themselves by hunting and gathering.

I will pitch my tent near the Bambuti huts, not far from a Balese village in the second-growth forest called Kwakwa. The great virgin forest with its immense trees is called Meli-Hetu; Bahana has camped there where it is cooler and more majestic. Now I hope to understand these people better. When I sit among them in the evening by the fire their tongues will wag more freely. Almost all the Bambuti speak a dialect of Swahili, so we can understand each other easily.

Hisa is a touchy character, the least thing annoys him. He can spend hours pouting. He goes with his wife into their hut or into the forest, lights a fire and smokes *chanvre*—marijuana—for hours. His wife Okahehu is even less pleasant, especially when she shouts. No one pays attention to their scenes. Today they are jealous of Bahana, to whom I have given some cigarettes and salt. It will soon be forgotten.

This evening there is a full moon, and dancing in Hisa's camp. I sit near the fire among the Bambuti, surrounded by forest, night, and mist. The light is greenish and strange. Women have ornamented their faces and bodies with paints made of forest plants, crushed and mixed with a little water. Each gives free rein to her imagination and the designs vary greatly: dots, circles, and lozenges in black and white. The men wear bunches of leaves in their belts.

Angalikiyana is the best drum player in the group; he contributes much to the success of the dances. At first he feels for his rhythm; after a few falterings the theme emerges. With a vague, lost look, he gazes above the dancers, one hand striking in cadence, the fist or the palm. The other hand holds a stick and follows the beat, tapping the top or side of the drum to produce sounds that are vibrant or dry. It takes a while before everyone is possessed with the magic of the rhythm. The drum, carved from a tree trunk, is covered with elephant hide, and from time to time the dance is interrupted to dry the skin at the fire as it becomes lax with the dampness of the night.

Everything of any importance at all is expressed in dance, be it sad or gay: the full moon, a death, a birth, a successful hunt, the coming of a friend. Thus the Pygmies free themselves from care—an illness, a spell, a quarrel—or let out the full force of their joy. All ages mix together, even very old women like Gana, Bahana's aged wife. The Bambuti tell me, "One dances as one drinks, as one eats—it is a necessity."

To watch them is delightful. Each gesture is lively and graceful; one feels their joy in living. Men and women together, they turn about

Maheme, wife of Citonu, has marked her face with a pattern drawn in vegetable pigment and has adorned her pierced nose and ears with tiny, scentless flowers. A little girl receives similar decoration. The designs, applied for the pleasure of being beautiful, have no set form or ritual meaning.

Angalikiyana, their bodies gleaming with sweat. Some of the men carry a carved flute hung around the neck by a strip of animal skin; into these they blow from time to time, producing a strange, almost hallucinatory sound.

I consider the varied personalities of this group. Hisa's father was the chief and left a great name as hunter and ladies' man. It seems he even had some success with the Balese girls, but he took an Mbuti wife, for he could never have paid the dower that a Mulese would ask for his daughter. He had five sons.

The eldest was Angalikiyana, "he who is always young." He has a reputation for being disagreeable, perhaps a bit crazy, but follows me faithfully everywhere. Normally he would have been chief.

Next is Hisa, then Manguna, smiling and friendly, who is bearded and extremely hairy. He and his old wife, Makubi, have built their hut some hundred yards away from the others. I asked them why: "We like peace, and the others spend their time squawking."

In fact the Bambuti make plenty of noise. You can hear them from far off wrangling, singing, whistling into their flutes. I think sound reassures them in the great silence of the forest.

Then there is Kwede-Kwede the cripple, very robust in spite of the withered leg which does not keep him from being a fine hunter. The fifth brother is Tikboro-Tikboro; clearly younger than the others, he seems deeply in love with his wife Tobo, whom he follows everywhere. This morning when the women went to the Isehe River to look for crabs, he was the only man to go along.

The Bambuti are individualists; each does what he wants when he wants to, most of the time. For instance, Bwana Simba decided to leave his group; he told no one. Everybody thought this perfectly natural. One day when he felt like it, he would come back. This does not preclude a certain cohesion: Big decisions like changing camp or setting out to hunt are made unanimously and carried out by the whole community. This is necessary for survival.

Relations with the Balese are quite friendly, and much more sharply defined than in the past. Some 30 years ago when the Pygmies needed food grown by the Balese, they simply took it from the fields and gardens, leaving meat in exchange. Now each Mbuti family head has a Mulese patron who gives him weapons and iron utensils made by the village smith. This equipment includes a spear, a knife—often just a large nail flattened at the end—and arrowheads, also used for cutting meat, shaving, and catching lice. In addition the Pygmy gets a hunting dog and such food as bananas, manioc, peanuts, maize, papayas, and sugarcane. In exchange he gives his patron part of each animal killed with these weapons.

In the Ituri, Bantu villages follow a common plan: a street lined with houses of sun-dried clay and leaf-covered roofs. Behind these stretch garden plots—including stands of marijuana, although growing it is illegal. Often one meets Pygmies who have come to get *malofu*, palm wine, or some marijuana. Bahana once told me, "Chanvre is our strength, what would we do without it? It makes our blood sparkle, our hearts to know no fear. It is like palm wine, it makes us happy."

I asked what would happen in a big *palabre,* or dispute, between a patron and a Pygmy. Surprised at such a question, he answered: "The Mulese would take back his lance and his dog, and what would the Mbuti do without his weapons? He would have to look for a new patron." On the other hand, if the patron treats his Mbuti badly, the latter will simply disappear into the forest until the matter blows over.

Tomorrow we are going to shift camp. Not for any dispute, but because the hunters are returning empty-handed, the game is timid, the mushrooms are scarce, the women have to go farther and farther to fill their baskets. The camp has been here two months, the huts are getting leaky, and it's boring to stay long in the same place. We need not go far; the forest is rich in sustenance for those who know how to find it, and the Pygmies never go very far from the Bantu villages.

Packing is easy. First, the weapons—every man carries his bow and arrows. Often he has his flute hung around his neck and his spear in his hand: no other baggage. The women have baskets of woven palm leaves, carried on the back with the aid of a strap passed across the forehead. Usually the basket contains a little cooking pot of aluminum or baked clay, obtained in a village, and the husband's water pipe. One or two will carry a mortar for making arrow poison. Someone will have a hammer made from the end of an elephant's tusk. This is used to beat fig bark for the loincloths that men make and women decorate. The tap-tap-tap of these hammers is characteristic of Pygmy camps. The women carry a knife thrust into the belt, ready to hand. As they walk, they cut down fruits or leaves or dig out edible tubers or larvae. Children follow the adults, the big girls carrying their little brothers or sisters on their backs. Boys carry their bows.

After about an hour's walking in the Meli-Hetu, we come to the new campsite near the Isehe River. The men start a clearing where the forest is not too dense. They cut only the undergrowth and only enough to squeeze in their huts. Meanwhile the women look for long, limber sticks. These they plant in a circle and weave into a dome-shaped trellis. To this frame they attach large leaves called *mongongo* for a watertight roof. Leafy branches piled on the ground serve as beds. The Bambuti have no bedclothes. They keep a fire burning near them all night for the forest is cool and damp, and the smoke helps drive off mosquitoes.

In two hours the camp is ready. Cooking fires are lighted before the huts. The women begin to prepare food gathered on the way. Some bring bananas obtained from the Balese. The day is nearly done, everyone is tired, all is still. We chat quietly. Tomorrow there will be a hunt; we start at daybreak.

The hunt shapes a great part of the life of the Bambuti. They live so close to the forest creatures that they notice their least movement. Often they track their quarry. The long, slender points of their arrows —some of forged iron, others of hard wood—are engraved with spirals to hold poison extracted from the roots of a liana. Its effect is quite rapid, but varies according to the severity of the wound. The hunters follow their prey until it dies. *(Continued on page 149)*

Rich in recreations, Bambuti culture cheerfully lacks material possessions. Even drums—the heartbeat of the dance—come from Bantu villages, but they answer the fervor of Pygmy musicians. Adu strikes his elephant-hide drum with hand or stick, producing a great variety of sound. Women play special dance-games. At left, they use a liana turned like a jump rope, the dancer keeping time to chants as she passes through the loop. Okahehu, Hisa's wife, turns for Maheme; Makubi, Manguma's wife, and Kehusi with her children look on laughing. Smoking —tobacco or marijuana— pleases all, though the men smoke more. Sitting with Hisa's children, the man at left has a bamboo pipe; a lightly bearded elder smokes a water pipe of gourd. Both pipes have clay bowls with charcoal laid atop. Marijuana comes from the Bantu gardens—illegal, cheap, and easy to get.

Intent on the chase, archers clamber down the cascades of the Isehe, hunting the mboloko, a small antelope that haunts the banks. Above, Hisa (in a Bantu hat) and his friends apply poison to new wooden arrows with fire-hardened tips. Below, they share the game, an mboloko. The Bantu patron who supplied the hunter's spear will get a thigh; Bahana— sporting his genet-fur headdress—gets a thigh also; Sokombili hands a foreleg to his little son; the man who made the kill will dispose of the rest.

In the camps, women construct the huts and tend to the children and cooking. Above, young women and an elderly man watch over young-sters as smoke from fires inside the huts—kept alight to discourage insects and to preserve the fire itself—filters through the roofs. At lower right, Okahehu sets plantains to boil. Meals are movable feasts, and anyone

can grill a snack. At left,
Tobo, the beloved wife of
Tikboro-Tikboro, roofs
their new hut with
mongongo *leaves.*

This morning the weather is dull, the forest still bathes in its white mists. I set out with Hisa's and Bahana's groups—they often hunt together. In the right hand old Bahana holds his spear, in the left a burning torch. He explains proudly to me that he is keeper of the fire, an important role. He follows the hunt, and wherever it stops—to rest or to grill some bananas or sweet potatoes—he revives the fire with a few twigs or a bit of his loincloth.

Suddenly, in front of me, Tikboro-Tikboro freezes. Before I have seen a thing, an arrow flies whistling and then another. If the arrows kill, good; if they miss—as in this case—they are picked up with great gusts of laughter. As these little men advance single file through the forest, some dance and some leap up to hang from lianas for sport.

Women and children come along too; they drive animals toward the hunters by making lots of noise. Boys of six or older use the bow. Some tell me that they have already killed a bird or the little antelope called *mboloko,* the blue duiker.

Today the hunters kill only one mboloko, but no one is upset. Tomorrow or some other day will be better.

Frequently an Mbuti waits alone, hidden, for a creature to pass. The Pygmies can imitate perfectly the call of the female mboloko. This may bring the male to investigate, for these little animals live in pairs. I want to observe this, but Atuka and Asani tell me, "Strengthen your heart. Sometimes a leopard answers the cry of the mboloko."

When we return to camp the duiker is divided. If an Mbuti kills an animal with a weapon of his own, he keeps the meat to be cooked for himself and his own family. If he uses a weapon provided by his Mulese patron, he gives the latter a back and a thigh. I ask what happens to the skins—"We eat the skin, it's very good."

Next morning I wake early and find the camp already busy. Young people are singing and talking. Women are reviving the fires under their pots. Suddenly I hear a violent quarrel. The Bambuti express their emotions very freely; at the least provocation they exchange rough abuse and personal insults. This quarrel arose over division of an antelope Asumani killed this morning with his own wooden arrows.

In the afternoon the sky grows leaden; a great storm is coming. The Bambuti are frightened and anxious. Families hurry to shelter, each to its own hut. Quickly they add leaves to the roofs; they build up the fires that had been banked with ashes—will the smoke perhaps hold off the thunderbolts? Suddenly the storm is upon us, violent and terrible. Lightning strikes a great tree about 50 yards away, tearing off long strips of wood. People whisper. I ask Sokombili, a young man who is usually smiling, "Why are you so afraid of the storm?"

"All this is in the order of things," he answers. "The thunderbolt sees the great red centipede in the tree and hurls itself from the sky and with its teeth and claws it gnaws and tears the tree. This always happens when the red centipede is around." Rain falls in heavy torrents and the storm passes over. The red centipede is one of many spirits that people the folklore of the Bambuti.

Night falls and the moon rises. Again there is calm. I sit beside

Apahosa, son of Atuka, has killed nine wild boars with this spear, the weapon used against elephants. A brave man and a great hunter, he often takes the game trails alone. Somewhat taller and sturdier than other Pygmies, Apahosa may have Bantu blood. White designs show mourning for a kinsman. His dog, provided by a Bantu patron, wears a wooden bell to guide its master in the chase, for it does not bark.

Bahana, Atuka, and Angalikiyana. It is not cold, but we have a fire. I ask Angalikiyana, the best elephant hunter in the region, to tell me how he got the terrible scars all over his body. He says he has twice been charged by a maddened elephant he had wounded. Once he had his thigh torn, the other time his back and chest were gouged.

This hunt is very dangerous. A Pygmy works his way up close to the elephant, hoping that the first blow of his short and heavy spear will hamstring the animal or hit a vital spot. The other hunters rush in and try to wound it again. They will follow the elephant for several days if necessary. If the elephant dies, the man who gave the first wound has the right to a foot and a thigh.

On other evenings they tell me fables and legends. Arms waving, hands twisting, they imitate the sounds and voices of beasts and of spirits who answer them—it is a lively dialogue between inhabitants of the forest. With great relish they tell me how an Mbuti first obtained fire, stealing it from a *Shetani*, a demon. Although the Shetani had eyes in the back of his head, the Pygmy distracted him with all sorts of games and escaped with the fire. The Bambuti received it with great joy, and since that day they have never let it go out.

As the storytellers repeat their tales, Atuka rocks his little sleeping son on his knees. One often sees men with children in their arms. They are extremely patient with them. Asani's boy is playing with a plastic wallet that Asani prizes highly. But rather than thwart the child, who howls when anyone tries to take it away, they let him destroy it.

Children have a good life, and are not kept apart from the adults. At about five, boys are given little bows to practice hunting. They play about the camp hanging from lianas, swinging, climbing trees. At a school in Mulave village, there are a number of Balese children but no Pygmies at all. I ask why. My friends laugh: "An Mbuti never goes to school. We never stay long enough in the same place."

Yet, in addition to skills of hunting, a Pygmy must master the truths of a spiritual world peopled by all sorts of beings of varying importance. "Real life" is so intimately linked to supernatural life that it is impossible to dissociate the two. In many forms, the spirits of the dead are always present, intervening constantly in the fate of the living.

When a man of Hisa's clan dies, his *boru'e'i*, or breath, is sometimes embodied in a leopard—his totem. Bahana explains that some of their ancestors had the power of transforming themselves into leopards. They went into the forest to call up the spirits, and leopard fur sprang out all over their bodies. In this guise they could go and eat the Balese's goats, or rid themselves of enemies. Other clans have totems: animals, or tree stumps, or even termite mounds.

I question Bahana and Atuka and other old men of Hisa's clan about their beliefs. They say that the forest is full of Shetanis and other spirits. "What are Shetanis like?" I ask Bahana. "Sometimes they take human or animal shapes," he replies, "but can you describe your shadow which changes all the time?"

First spirit is Kahini, father of all the Bambuti. As Atuka says, "He is to the Bambuti what roots are to a tree. He is our beginning, the sum of the breath of our ancestors." To appease the shades of the ancestors, one makes offerings to Kahini. If one is ill, or there is trouble in the clan, again one asks Kahini to intervene: "He looks after us."

Then there is Hefengi, the very small man who directs the Shetanis and creatures of the forest. Bahana tells me that it can be most unwise for a hunter to set out very early in the morning at first cockcrow, for he risks seeing Hefengi walking ahead of him as he haunts the forest in a loincloth of white bark. I ask if he is dangerous. "Of course," Bahana answers, "spirits represent the dead. Would you like to meet the breathing of death? It is terrifying."

"And the Toré, what do you think of it, Bahana?"

"The Toré," he said, "is completely different. It is alive. It is the spirit of the forest represented by living men. For it to keep its power and authority, it must stay hidden and mysterious."

On previous visits I had heard of the Toré, or Sumba, and thought it might be much the same ritual as that called Molimo among Pygmy net-hunters. I tried to find out from Bahana, Atuka, and Asani if the Toré might not visit their camp soon. They did not answer.

But some days later they told me that the Toré would come that very evening, and if I wanted to see it, I had only to go with them. I was astonished that they would let a woman be present, for Bambuti women may not see the Toré. When they hear it, they shut themselves in their huts with their children and put branches before the doors.

About five o'clock, Bahana, Atuka, Asani, and Bwana Simba came for me. The Toré lay in a little river over half a mile from the camp. They had already explained that this Toré is a trumpet between two and three yards long, made from the hollowed trunk of any slender tree; moisture keeps it from cracking and gives it a better tone.

We follow a little path across the forest; night falls. Suddenly I hear the groaning of the Toré; it is there, invisible but near. I ask to see it — an ordinary hollowed tree trunk. This trumpet represents nothing in itself; it is only the instrument that invokes the spirit Toré. Its importance resides in the mysteries that shroud these rites and the reactions they provoke. One calls the Toré in times of trouble. Its cries and its strange chants announce its presence, restoring order in the camp.

Young men take up the Toré and bear it before them on outstretched arms. They have wrapped it in leaves and small branches. Others carry their elephant spears and turn about us to give the illusion of a great beast charging in the forest. Sometimes they cross the camp in a rush, scattering everything they find in their path.

When the bearers stop, Asani blows into the trumpet and sings. His voice, entirely transformed, no longer conveys anything human. Easily one believes that the spirit of the forest is singing. The setting, the eerie atmosphere add to the unreality of the scene. Drums vibrate, earth trembles under the hammering of feet. Water pipes gurgle; the live coals sway to the cadence, little red gleams in the night.

The Toré prowls nearer and nearer the camp. Its weird and savage chant comes out of the depths of the forest, of the night, of time — now raucous, growling like a wild beast, now extraordinarily melodious.

All animals and demons keep silence. Awe fills the heart that hears the Toré, spirit of the Meli-Hetu. The men remaining in camp answer the Toré; they are drunk on marijuana and palm wine. Atuka's voice resounds powerfully for so small a man. He gives the beat, the others follow. The Toré sings and groans continually. Everyone dances and sings, improvising, elaborating a single note, a general theme. A drum speaks, stifled, breathy; another answers, tremulous, broken. All is rhythm, drums, the earth, the Toré, the forest, and each head, each body. Young Cepi is beside himself; he is the incarnation of the dance —a faun's silhouette lit by the moon, by the flames.

Now the Toré fades into the shadows. Its resonance and fullness pervade the forest. Until late, late in the night the men sing and dance. After this it is hard to get to sleep—but have I dreamed?

The day returns. I plan to walk through the forest to the Ituri, the great river that gives its name to the region. Biani, named chief of the Efe Pygmies by the Congolese government, goes with me. Often, with an ample wave of the hand encompassing the whole forest, he tells me, "All this is mine. All these people belong to me—they are many and everywhere." He wants above all to convince himself of his power.

As we go, he tells me his worries. "The main thing is, we were the first; this is our country. Our grandfathers and their grandfathers lived in this forest. We received the Balese like brothers. We showed them the wealth of the forest. Now they treat us like slaves. They don't respect my authority as great chief." Then he tells me about his projects to bring the Pygmies out of the forest, set them to raising crops, and put them near the main roads so that tourists can see them more easily. I try to explain that the visitors come to see the Pygmies because they are not like other Africans, and that he should not try to make his people give up their customs and the traditions of their ancestors.

Earlier plans to settle the Bambuti as farmers met no success. It requires a strong habit of foresight and painstaking work to raise a crop. Moreover, if the Pygmies are placed in villages, they will be deprived of their true country. Their huts are not made to withstand the implacable sun of clearings where all the trees are cut to let gardens grow. And why take so much trouble when Balese fields can provide?

If the Pygmies leave their forest the three great Bantu tribes will quickly begin to absorb them. The Bambuti ask a ridiculously small dower for their daughters. The Bantu know this; the day may come when a young Mbuti who wants to marry will not find a wife.

When at night I listen to the ominous cries of the hyrax, I imagine this forest peopled by timid and mysterious animals: the okapi, the bongo, pangolins, snakes with skins like the most sumptuous of Oriental carpets. I tell myself that if I believed that some of these creatures were possessed by the soul of my ancestors, by demons, by spirits, I should feel oppressed, disquieted. But the Bambuti remain gay and carefree; it seems not to weigh upon them.

What is to become of these small people—how long can they preserve their ancestral traditions? How long will they continue to wander, engulfed in their immense and magnificent forest?

At home in the virgin forest called Meli-Hetu, two boys explore the runners of a great liana. A place of danger and foreboding to the Bantu farmer, the forest is the trusted and loved environment of the Pygmy nomad. It gives him food and shelter for the gathering, sharpens his wits with the hunt. Its might teaches him awe, and always its abundance sustains him.

Tools shouldered, Guajiro salt harvesters end work in the red dawn on the coast of Colombia's Guajira Peninsul

Touchy and Self-sufficient as Their
GUAJIROS *Toughen on the Scrubland*

By Loren McIntyre
Illustrations by the Author

Money they earn here twice yearly goes for newly learned luxuries and for necessities—like these shovels.

Own Goats,
They Wander

Map labels:
Caribbean Sea
Cabo de la Vela
Manaure
Puerto López
Maicao
Barranquilla
Maracaibo
VENEZUELA
COLOMBIA
SOUTH AMERICA

Bright manta *swirls to northeast trade winds as a young Guajiro woman shovels salt crystals to help fill 130-pound sacks for 13 cents each.*

OUR JEEP CRAWLED out of a gulley, an oven, and paused at the desert's rim. One set of ruts zigged right and another zagged left. Which led to the salt harvest? Instead of pointing the way as usual, my Guajiro Indian guide Germán Pushaina put on my sunglasses and cap. *"Soy gringo,"* he declared impishly. *"Usted busque el camino.* You find the way." Jesting aside, Germán was challenging my familiarity with his territory, La Guajira.

I took stock, turning my back to the afternoon sun and the Sierra Nevada de Santa Marta, highest snowpeaks in Colombia. Far behind me lay Ríohacha, a wizened coastal town once plundered by Drake and Hawkins, where mothers still discipline their children with a 400-year-old threat: "Be quiet or Drake will eat you!" Ahead, the Guajira Peninsula jutted a hundred miles into the northeast trades that ruffle the Caribbean along the top of South America. The right-hand ruts led into cactus forest—populated by goat-herding nomads—which stretched to the Gulf of Venezuela. The left-hand tracks ran into a shimmering mirage with a donkey caravan upside down in the middle of it. "Let's bear left," I decided, "then follow the beach to the harvest."

Germán grinned. *"Dicho como si fuera Pushaina.* Said like a member of the Pushaina clan." He touched his clan totem, a peccary carved on the grip of a .38 pistol stuck in his belt. Many Guajiros carry arms; whether for show or in anticipation of clan warfare I could never be sure. Two decades' experience among deferential Andean Indians hadn't prepared me for the arrogance of the Guajiros. Their unwillingness to speak Spanish limited my understanding even after I learned enough of their language to gain a measure of acceptance—or at least to diminish their hostility. Fortunately Germán had no language prejudice. He considered himself *civilizado*—he wore pants—and he was merely jaunty while his country cousins were brash. Germán was my trustworthy friend but by no means a man Friday.

Caked with dust, we arrived after dark at Manaure, terminus of a ten-mile expanse of coastal salt pans. The night sparkled with campfires, as if an army had bivouacked in the nearby sands. We prowled from one camp to another until greeted with cries of *"Antsh pía! Kazáchiki, waré!* You've come! What's new, friend!" Out of the shadows came Miguel, Barranquilla, and Emiro, men married into the Epieyú clan, whose friendship I'd won during a previous harvest. Women touched my arm, asking, "What have you brought me, waré?"

I broke out tinned meat, a bolt of bright cloth to make *mantas* (women's square-cut gowns), and yarn to make pompons for *guayucos* (men's aproned G-strings). I gave the gifts to tiny Rita Epieyú, Miguel's wife, custodian of the family's food and finances as well as its surname. As Guajiro society is matrilineal, Rita's and Miguel's children are Epieyú. Their daughters Blanca and Telemina prepared our meal.

The camp lay open to the sky. Hammocks swung from scrubby trees. Pots and saddles dangled from stubs of branches. Clamped to a stump

A frequent contributor to the Society's publications, LOREN MCINTYRE *first visited Latin America in 1935, made his home there for 17 years.*

At daybreak Guajiros labor on their salt pans, where sea water
evaporates under the tropic sun. Twice a year they gather near Manaure
to harvest salt—much as their ancestors did before the Spanish came.

With taunts and teasing counter-steps, chichamaya dancers dodge to the beat of a snare drum, the girl's hood and manta billowing and pompons bobbing from the man's aproned guayuco. The author's guide, Germán, in "civilized" clothes, walks to the visitors' bower. Below, a girl shakes a

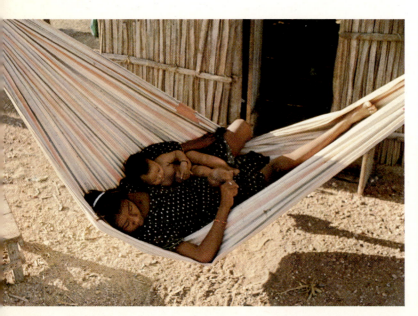

maraca to soothe a baby; an older woman leads a donkey pulling water in an old rum barrel.

was a cast-iron food grinder, sign of a family whose main sustenance is corn gruel, *újor*. While the women rigged our hammocks, I drove to the Concesión de Salinas headquarters to find out when the salt harvest might begin.

"Not until next week," advised technical director Alvaro Ortega Ortega. "Crystals have formed but we have yet to drain the brine."

But at 2 a.m. I awoke to find the camp deserted. I ran to the levee. Under a full moon hundreds of Guajiros were sprinkled upon two 100-acre cakes of salt deposited by the evaporation of sea water. They worked their claims in ghostly silence, ankle-deep in brine. Women in mantas broke the crust with iron-tipped shafts. Tall bare-legged men with pompons bobbing at their hips shoveled the crystals into piles.

Along the levee straggled a dozen soldiers with automatic rifles. "*¿Qué pasa?*" I asked. "Did the Guajiros jump the gun?"

"*Sí, Doctor,* while we full up sleep, here they come," answered the squad leader, practicing his English. "*Tres mil chinos,* ladies and mens, wiz dangers pick and shovel. Us city guys bad prepare for war in this misery hot place. Anyway, I call halt or everybody shoots." He waved his arms, describing the midnight invasion by a thousand Indians along a nebulous mile-wide front, some making rude gestures and shouting indecencies as they filtered past the soldiers and settled on the salt like flies on sugar. He laughed with nervous embarrassment. "What for I call halt, *hombre*? They don't even espeak espanish!"

"Except when they feel like it," I added. The sergeant shrugged. "*¡Que cosechen!* Let them harvest!"

I found the family far out on the salt. In the dark I hardly recognized Rita Epieyú and her daughters; their faces were painted black to guard against wind and glare when the sun came up. Barranquilla and Emiro were filling sacks from the mounds of salt. Together, they hoisted one upon Rita's skinny back and helped adjust her headstrap. The birdlike grandmother staggered 200 yards through the brine again and again to dump the 130-pound bags on the levee.

The east burst with color. Indians began to shoulder their shovels and head for their hammocks. As if crayoned by a child, the sun stood on edge an instant on the sand. Then, just as foretold in Guajiro legend, the trade winds caught the red disk and whirled it overhead.

But for the sea breeze sweeping the waterfront, 51-year-old Miguel could not have labored so furiously under the ascending sun. Stripped to his guayuco, the husky grandfather was easy to spot in a column of slim bearers jogging down a pier with sacks of salt on their heads. With a flick of his neck and a thrust of both arms, he arched the sack far into a barge used to ferry salt to a ship anchored offshore. Every day Miguel alone hand-delivered more than 30 tons for conversion at Cartagena into chemicals for Colombia's burgeoning industry.

Dr. Ortega approached with a gesture of resignation. "Can't expect disciplined behavior; they grow up so footloose and fancy-free. They even set their own work quotas. With the 500th bag, those bearers will quit and go to spend the day in their hammocks—where they're conceived, born, nursed, live, and die. They want to take over new ponds we're bulldozing down the coast, but except for two pans traditionally theirs, our entire operation is automated. Manual harvesting is vastly more costly. Yet the twice-a-year trek to the salt harvest is a mainstay of Guajiro culture and we have to inject some cash into their economy. The Concesión pays 13 cents a sack. Goats are great for buying a wife but a bit awkward when paying for a spool of thread."

We pondered the anomaly of the Guajiros in Colombia's headlong development. I mentioned my old friend, Capt. Alvaro Sanchez, a Guajiro who currently leads the nation's helicopter school. "They learn fast when they have a chance," mused Dr. Ortega. "Now that employment opportunities induce more families to settle near towns, more children go to school. The few who get to the big cities are swept into the mainstream of national life and seldom return. Did you know a Guajiro once ran for Vice President of Colombia?"

He wondered about education for nomads in their own environment. Recalling that few Guajiro children seem to attend the one-room rural schools where a local *maestra* teaches all three grades, I said, "Formal schooling doesn't reach those whose habits are really nomadic — or *andariego.*" Andariego means "roving," a term some authorities use for the Guajiros. Anthropologists have classified these Indians as seminomadic, "temporary nomads," or "occasional migrants," for their activities fit no standard pattern. At our camp, relatives — cousins, aunts, uncles — came and went so casually and continually that I never did determine the size of Rita's family.

One day after the harvest a trucker offered the family a cut-rate ride to their habitat near Jachina, somewhere in the middle of the northern peninsula. Within 20 minutes they had broken their two-month-old camp and departed. Germán assured me he could track them. I hoped so, because the *rancherías,* or hamlets, of the big Epieyú clan are dispersed in five distinct zones throughout 3,600 square miles occupied by about 44,000 Guajiro Indians. A much smaller number of whites, mestizos, and Negroes are concentrated in a few towns.

Germán and I sped over hard sand, picking whatever tracks suited our fancy or making our own along the shore of the Spanish Main. A gale ripped spume from the green Caribbean. We passed great mounds of oyster shell, monuments to past centuries when Guajiro pearl divers helped adorn Europe's noblewomen. Ahead loomed a promontory named Cabo de la Vela. Guajiros call the region Jepira and believe their dead wander or abide thereabouts. Short of the cape, in a blinding dust storm, Germán announced, "Here they turned inland." How could he tell from a maze of crisscrossed tire ruts with no landmarks visible? I never learned.

At twilight, on high and desolate ground beyond Jachina, we approached a scattering of shacks. "Kazáchiki, waré?" To signify that we were welcome, the women hung hammocks in the visitors' bower, an open-sided shelter, and brought mugs of újor. I wondered where they'd gotten the water to make it. Of 600 windmills and wells in the Guajira, we hadn't seen a single one the past four hours.

I found out next morning when the boys drove 300-odd goats to a

Fastidious Telemina, a daughter of the Epieyú clan, wears black manta and face paint with elegance. Paint once showed a woman's age and status, still shields her eyes and skin from the glaring sun.

jagüey (pronounced "hagh-way"), a pond 100 yards long, ringed with shade trees. Years ago the Colombian government began bulldozing jagüeys in upper Guajira to hold the autumn rains. The nearest one held a stagnant green liquid scarcely suitable for a hog wallow.

Rita's middle-age nieces, Ligia and Genoveva, fed Germán and me in return for favors such as trucking them to a distant jagüey which was deep enough to tap sweet water. They would load the jeep with 15 or 20 water jugs and empty cooking-oil cans.

I wondered why the family lived so far from water. Germán pointed out that ponds and wells attract members of other clans, riders from distant regions, bathers, herders, and vagrants who might cause trouble. "At isolated ranchos everyone is related and there is less risk of *purchi,* a showdown between the clans."

One stifling afternoon Emiro slaughtered several kids and Barranquilla began to beat a big snare drum. Scores of relatives and friends rode up on donkeyback and horseback, dressed in their best mantas and guayucos. *"Chichamaya?"* I asked. *"Si, hombre."* At last I would see the famous Guajiro ceremonial dance, the chichamaya. "What's the occasion?" "For *tránsito,"* answered Germán.

Tránsito means "traffic" in Spanish and I presumed they were celebrating the opening of a road or purchase of a truck. I hadn't yet learned of Rita's third daughter—reared by an aunt—whose social name was Tránsito. (I never found out the private name of any Guajiro, even Germán's, as it is spoken only by the mother's immediate family. Many Guajiros use yet a third, baptismal name.)

Then, at the door of a hut where she had been confined over a year, Tránsito appeared, looking for all the world like a Japanese doll. Her skin was pallid, accented with rouge and lipstick. Her straight black hair, frequently shorn during internment, now stood out stiffly. Her flowered manta was new and ankle-length, adult. She wore a grown-up gold necklace and ring, for her girlhood had been cast away. She looked shy. Now she knew female secrets of love and motherhood and household management which her Aunt Antonia had taught her during the seclusion that began with her first menstruation. At last were ended the months of drinking herbs to regurgitate her childhood ways and to help shape her figure. Gone were the dark days of weaving and waiting in the closed shelter. She was reborn. She had a new name. Tránsito was ready for her "coming out" party.

At nightfall the chichamaya dance began. Fueling his nerve with firewater, a young newcomer snatched off his hat and waved it high. Dancing backward in a circle, he challenged the girls to catch him. For a while, none came forward. Then Telemina lifted a billowing hood over her head and shoulders and danced in pursuit, trying to step on his feet and send him sprawling. She flew like a lovely bird, catching the trade winds in her hood, but the youth danced backward even more swiftly, teasing Telemina. "Send your little sister if you can't catch me." And soon Tránsito was flying after the young man.

She danced with other youths before the fiesta waned, and I suppose she wondered which of them might someday offer her parents a

Fishermen for generations, the Guajiros exploited their coast in pre-Conquest times. Above, a man mends a wide-meshed turtle net; sun-dried turtle is a standby food. A boy displays a fine female spiny lobster laden with red eggs. The Indians like lobster but sell many: a legal trade with Bogotá, a matter of smuggling with Aruba.

great herd of goats for her hand in marriage. I wondered why the Guajiros practice no comparable rites for young men.

By midyear the thirsty sun had reduced jagüeys around Jachina to slimy wallows. Tiptoeing goats had stripped the *mapua* trees as high as the tallest billy could reach. It was time to drive the herds to the Serranía de Jarara, to let them forage in less desiccated highlands.

But where were the men? Barranquilla had found a job in the big coastal city 200 miles away from which he took his name, Blanca's husband was picking cotton in the lower Guajira, others were fishing for sea turtles. Yet when Rita fell sick, complaining of chills, the men reappeared in two to four days, dropping everything to attend to her. Nothing is more important to the clan than the well-being of every member. But how did they get the news, without drums or telegraph? Even Germán failed to explain it. As there is no *piache* (medicine man) or doctor in Jachina, women had asked me for medicines and begged me to pray for Rita—most gringos who come this way are either doctors or missionaries. The men finally dispelled Rita's chills by building a small fire under her hammock.

Little by little the men, boys, and goats left for the hills. One morning before daybreak I opened an eye to see Ligia applying travel paint from forehead to chin and Genoveva packing her best manta and a sequined handbag. Girls were saddling donkeys. My jeep was draped with water jugs, bows and arrows, and small boys.

When the jeep and donkey cavalcade took off for the Jarara hills, I was the only one who waved goodbye to Rita, Miguel, and the small children left behind. Farewells seem unnecessary among these people who constantly come and go. Once under way, our cast of characters changed continually, dropping off a rider at this stop and picking up a cousin at the next. We detoured around territory of unfriendly clans. I'd have become hopelessly lost without Germán. Usually we slept at a rancho—a single-family home—of the Epieyú clan, identifiable by the king vulture some men had tattooed on their forearms.

A few dwellings are stout adobe houses; others have neither walls nor roofs. Aged couples and adolescent girls usually live in small cane-slatted huts. Although I saw no vestiges of the slavery still common 20 years ago when vanquished clans lost their freedom in bloody feuds, I did chance upon a teen-ager chained by her neck to a tree "because she misbehaved," said Germán. Another day I saw a boy hung by his heels and spun at the end of a rope until he retched, which Germán explained was punishment for running away.

Sometimes I heard shouts as youngsters dashed into the scrub with bows and arrows, following tracks invisible to my eye. Another yell and some skinny child on a dead run would let fly an arrow, skewering a skittering wild thing. On lucky days we dined on rabbit, which I much preferred to sun-dried kid or jet-black jerky of sea turtle.

In the evenings the men and women insisted on listening to cassette tapes of Guajiro songs and verses I'd recorded. Newcomers sang pentatonic solos, always ending with a grunt. By 7 p.m. black twists of smoking *tabaco* burned out and the camp slept.

Pans began to rattle at 2 a.m. and by 3 everyone's hammock was stuffed into its net bag. If I hadn't finished my gringo chores—like brushing teeth, cleaning cameras, and shaving—before the first flare of red in the east, my companions would look at the sky and reproachfully remark, "We've lost half the day."

We crossed highlands far more desolate than the cactus flats of central Guajira. "The only signs of life around here," Germán remarked, "are those tombs." He referred to small white buildings clustered on hillocks, each with a white cross above a gabled roof. One evening I noticed lights flickering on a mountainside. Germán said a man had just been buried. "His people are lighting trails leading west so his spirit can find its way to Cabo de la Vela and not torment their dreams."

Since Blanca was pregnant, her husband rode ahead to watch for snakes or sights of death that might endanger her or the child. If her first-born died, she would have to be secluded for months as at puberty. Luckily she wasn't with us when we came upon an old woman and a girl emptying a preliminary grave. The woman removed bones from their hammock shroud while the girl reverently dusted them and dropped them into a pottery urn for ritual interment in a nearby clan tomb. When I tried to take pictures, the old woman screamed and flew at me with her pick. Germán fended her off.

"She says her brother's grave will remain open in your picture; his soul will never rest. She says you must surrender the photo and pay 1,000 pesos." Fifty dollars! By now I was accustomed to Guajiro hostility toward photographers and demands for enormous payments. I settled the old woman's claim by dropping my exposed film into the urn and paying only 20 pesos for my offense.

Nowhere on the trek did we encounter public officials. Justice in those hills follows Guajiro tradition of *cobro* and *pago*, charge and payment. All torts, crimes, bad advice, and wrongful deaths of people or animals must be settled by payment to kin of the injured party. Unsettled claims are appealed to the clan. If clans fail to agree, they fight.

Homicide is the costliest crime. Speaking the name of the deceased is next—it reawakens grief. All bloodshed is expensive. A girl who cut her finger helping a woman of another clan once collected 4 goats, 5 pigs, 15 chickens, 25 skeins of yarn, and 5 bars of soap. Germán stressed the importance of blood as the link of the clan and the basis for matrilineage. "About one's mother, there can be no doubt; and it has to be her blood of which one is made, as that blood is no longer spilled with every moon once the little little man is planted by who knows what father. No one carries a father's blood in his body."

A Guajiro usually buys his wife from another clan. Bargaining might begin with, say, 30 goats. Payment establishes her worth and serves as a money-back guarantee of wifely performance. A husband may return an unfaithful wife to her family and recover all animals paid for her plus pago for the offense. The wife's family may then demand payment from the adulterer equal to the value of the dowry!

As women tarried and men disappeared, I suspected that one motive for this journey—as with much Guajiro wandering—was social,

Flimsy shelters cast evening shadows across the clearing of an Epieyú ranchería, or hamlet of several families. At right, goats leave a rough corral of branches for a water hole; at one, a transplanted bathtub serves as a trough for water raised by a windmill. Below, at left, a palisade of cactus keeps chickens, goats, and pigs from the kitchen area where Genoveva, sometimes the author's hostess, prepares a meal with a pot of ujór, corn gruel, at her side.

Celebrating Easter, girls in their best mantas stroll in the garden of a Capuchin mission called Nazareth, where Guajiro pupils may complete the elementary grades. The school receives more girls than boys. Since tribal custom isolates girls at puberty, some spend their time of seclusion training here. The hammocks they weave — more decorative than the ordinary — may sell for $75 apiece.

especially after we'd left the Serranía de Jarara and were reaching the Gulf of Venezuela. We followed naked dunes down the coast to Puerto López. Here a bit of fallout from smuggling supplies the region with American detergents, Italian antibiotics, and Scotch whiskey.

As we neared Maicao, where Germán grew up, his stories began to sound like a-girl-in-every-port escapades. He has more than one wife and family, but doesn't keep them all under the same bower. His retreat from the open polygamy of his guayuco-wearing brothers may have something to do with the cross he wears on a gold necklace.

Maicao seems plucked from the sands of a Mediterranean country. Most of its shopkeepers are Arabs. In places with exotic names like Almacén Fátima de Mohamed Charenek they sell their wares to flowing-robed Guajiro women and old men dressed for town in the bygone costume of baggy knee-length skirts and open-crowned turbans.

Genoveva and Ligia wanted to see a doctor, shop, and call on relatives in Venezuela. Eager to reach the limits of Guajiro territory, I took them along. A few minutes from Maicao I checked in at the border. Formalities cost me 30 minutes of red tape while dozens of Guajiros came and went without stopping. For them no boundary exists. Colombia and Venezuela recognize Guajiros as citizens of both countries with no need of the documents required of all others.

Venezuela looked prosperous but fenced in. Palms and cornfields lined the highway. I saw no goats. We came to supermarkets, telephone poles, flat concrete and towering glass — we entered Maracaibo, now a city of 608,000. I dropped the ladies at the Guajiro quarter in the northern suburbs where most men consider themselves civilizados although their wives still wear mantas. Day laborers earn good pay here.

Everywhere in the peninsula I had heard praise of Venezuela's schools and welfare projects to ease the transition from nomadism to big-city life. "It's an enormous adjustment, full of family conflict," a social worker told me. "Buses replace donkeys, police supersede pago, and father-dominated households supplant the matrilineal clan structure with the full backing of the church and the nation's legal system. It's easy to see why women often remain at the rancho when their husbands go to the city."

I crossed a magnificent bridge over Lake Maracaibo, which blankets one of the world's richest oil fields. Thousands of derricks rise from the water, fencing the southeastern end of nomad territory just as definitely as snowpeaks of the Sierra Nevada mark the southwestern limits. A bit overwhelmed by the impact of steel and smoke, I hastened back to my hammock at Germán's rancho near Maicao.

Like Dr. Ortega, I still wondered about schools for nomads in their own environment. So I set out for an almost legendary institution hidden beyond the verdant peaks of the 2,500-foot Serranía de Macuira, near the end of the peninsula, two blistering days away. On Easter morning, 1971, I rolled into Nazareth, an oasis below the forested mountainside facing the northeast trades. Guajiro señoritas promenaded along cool pathways in richly colored mantas. Here and there a nun in immaculate white accented the changing pattern.

Capuchin priests from Spain founded the mission a half-century ago for children orphaned by clan warfare. Now it takes all the pupils it can, for the elementary grades. I asked to meet the Capuchin authors of my thumbworn Guajiro reference books. A bearded monk in a brown cassock dribbled a basketball in my direction. He said the Spanish scholars had left. "I'm Padre Bernardino from L'Aquila, northeast of Rome. Mind giving my boys a basketball lesson? Oh, I know . . . they're too individualistic to play as a team, but someday. . . ."

I begged off coaching and explained the National Geographic Society's interest in nomads. "Magnificent!" cried the padre. "We haven't a single map to show our young pathfinders where they're situated on this earth. Why, some think all outsiders belong to the same clan!" I promised to send wall maps of the Americas and the world.

He showed me the mission's elaborate wind-driven water-storage system, and large granaries for the rainy months when Nazareth's 300 boarders are totally isolated by washouts. At dinner he voiced a concern: "We receive 8,000 pesos a month from the Ministry of Education but $1.22 per student isn't enough without American help. Do you no longer have farm surplus? We try to raise our own crops but agriculture is almost impossible where goats abound." Padre Bernardino agrees with some scientists that goats, introduced from Europe four centuries ago, both caused and perpetuate nomadism. "Yet we cannot condemn goats—the nomads' capital, medium of exchange, main preoccupation—without a better idea."

Inside the convent wall Indian maidens strolled through gardens, all bubbling with fun except one pretty youngster lying in a grassy shadow with her face to the sky sobbing her heart out. "What's the matter?" I asked a white-habited sister who was picking out chords on a guitar. She whispered, "I must guard that she does not hang herself. It has happened . . ." "But why?" The sister touched her lips.

The Mother Superior told me Nazareth hoped to change the children from *Indio* to *civilizado*, from tribal to national culture. Yet elementary classes didn't provide careers and many graduates drifted back to Guajiro ways, ". . . to guayuco and manta," she said, wryly. "You see that girl crying? Well, she has to leave tomorrow, sold in marriage to a man she's met only once. He paid her maternal uncle well: 10 cows, 80 goats, 2,000 pesos cash, and his mother's gold jewelry." Worth at least $1,600. The mission respects Guajiro law in these matters.

"Oh, she won't hang herself, though she's tempted to do it to get even with her uncle by thus forcing him to return her dowry—and what's more, to pay a big cobro for her death. But Christian indoctrination has reinforced her Guajiro belief that such desperate action is wicked. Anyway, I think she's secretly pleased to learn she's worth so much! Almost always the girls are happy to follow their customs."

"Too bad her clan didn't send her to the city," observed the sister. "There she might have found a civilized husband."

But it was too late for her to keep house for a lord and master who would handle the money and give her children his surname. Now she was destined, like Rita Epieyú, to live under the stars of La Guajira.

Segregated by sex, boys eat in their own refectory at Nazareth mission. Empty benches and filled plates await youngsters quarantined for mumps, who will come later. For lack of space at the busy table, one child must eat alone. "We hope," says one of the monks, "to teach them to defend themselves against exploitation in civilized life."

Family herds of zebu cattle gather at a water hole in west-central Niger. During the winter drought, each Bororo

Assembling Each Year for a Season

BORORO Herdsmen of Niger Celebrate

By VICTOR ENGLEBERT
Illustrations by the Author

...ousehold will individually search for pastures and water until the next rainy season unites the people again.

of Dances,

the Rains

AFRICA

NIGER

In Waggeur · Agadez

Tchin Tabaraden · Abalak

Lake Chad

Niger R.

PROFILING ITSELF against the canopy of heaven, a circle of heads slowly turns around me. Of the hands clapping and of the feet sliding over the ground I see nothing, for it is night. The bodies move shoulder against shoulder and on each head quivers a black ostrich feather. From the darkness of the earth mounts a deep chant—born from the solitude of herdsmen under boundless skies—a chant that fills my head, leaving no space for thought.

In the sky the Milky Way stretches its vaporous scarf of gauze sewn with diamonds and pinned by constellations, Scorpius and Orion.

A dancer sings a few words alone, which the others repeat, and resumes his solo before the chorus dies away so that his voice seems to be reborn each time from the dying clamor.

Next to me an old woman points her finger at one of the dancing men. Obediently I light him with my flashlight. She scrutinizes him while he feigns complete indifference, then utters a shrill *yu-huu* to spur the circle into a better performance. To the unfortunates whose appearance does not meet the criteria of these nomads—figure tall and slim, forehead high and convex, nose and lips thin—she throws sarcastic words.

Imperceptibly the rhythm has changed, the dancers have passed to another chant. Half of the circle now sings something which the other half answers. The chants are monotonous, a few syllables interminably repeated. And they began in midafternoon and will resume tomorrow. Still they are beautiful and moving.

Night has swallowed the old crone; and my friend Mokao, who had left me alone in the middle of the circle, has come back. Silently he takes my hand in his. The star which he had shown me near the horizon at nightfall is now overhead. The fires are out. Already the savanna is dotted with bodies resting coiled on straw mats. Soon the last dancers will disperse into the night. I too retire and go lie under my tent, which the rainy season has forced upon me.

We are near the well and settlement of Tchin Tabaraden in the Republic of Niger, camped in the Azaouak, a savanna region bordering the Sahara and crushed under a heavy sun. It is the beginning of August and the grassy area, so hopelessly dry the rest of the year, is swept by storms that will last a few weeks and then rapidly die. Puddles and ponds glint in every depression, and a soft breeze makes the short green grass shiver in the cool mornings following nights of tornadoes. The acacia trees have hidden their long bone-colored thorns under a profusion of tiny green leaves.

Rains mark for my nomad companions a respite from long labor, from a quest as unrelenting as it is disappointing, sometimes from a long misery. With water and grass everywhere it is no longer necessary to pursue the horizon, each family on its own in search of ever rarer, scorched pastures, or to draw the parsimonious water of wells for the thirsty herds. The large red-brown cattle may drink alone and rich

Folds of a cotton blanket frame the tattooed face of a Bororo maiden. She wears all her finery— large hoops around the edge of each pierced ear, a homemade necklace of glass beads and metal trinkets—for dances in which she plays but a minor role: to admire the male participants.

Photojournalist VICTOR ENGLEBERT, *a veteran of desert marches with the Tuareg, reports on their sub-Saharan neighbors—and rivals.*

Lowering clouds darken the sky over the camp of the author's Bororo friend Mokao (above). His wife, daughters, and three visiting cousins wait for the rain near the leather-covered hut—a shelter unnecessary in the dry season. Tied between two stakes, a leather rope called a daangol tethers the calves to keep them from wandering, and to prevent them from nursing the cows dry. It also divides the camp: A wife takes charge from her calabash stand to the daangol; beyond spreads the domain of men. Between June and September, a brief wet season greens the savanna and replenishes water holes, easing the perennial struggle for survival. Marginal lands in the north can support more cattle; the Bororos congregate there to celebrate births and marriages and to conduct the all-important business of the herds. Then families give or lend cattle to kinsmen and others who have lost animals by disease, famine, or official fines, and to sons establishing households of their own. At left, dancers huddle under plastic sheets as a downpour forces them to shelter.

Demanding attention with a rough lick, one of Mokao's cows (above) returns the affection Bororos feel for their cattle. Kabo (below), 11-year-old son of Mokao, playfully fondles another cow's muzzle as he leads the family herd; for years he has known each animal by name. A

grasses allow great concentrations of herdsmen. It is the time of rest, meetings, of transactions in cattle, of dances and marriages.

But who are these Bororos? Of a stock scattered from the Atlantic to Lake Chad and speaking a language called Fulfulde, they are distinguished from the tribes among whom they live by their stiltwalker elegance, their delicate features, their light coppery skins, and, maybe most of all, by their association with herds of large zebus. Their origins themselves seem tied to their herds.

They belong to a great population known in English as Fulani, probably more than six million in all. They call themselves *Fulbe* (singular, *Pullo*). Some of their forebears founded pagan kingdoms in the tenth century; others, converted to Islam, ruled Moslem states that rose to the dignity of empire. Many settled in cities or villages or farms; but others, the pastoral Fulani, remained nomads. Among these, custom sets apart the *Bororo'en,* or Bororos, as a distinctive people.

Now the Bororos who wander in the merciless sun of Azaouak halt at village markets where they trade milk and butter for millet during the dry season. In the rainy season they move into the lands of the Tuareg when the latter migrate north for salt. They stubbornly reject outside influences to follow their ancestors' ways. They feel threatened, however. The Tuareg, no longer able to live by plunder, are slowly pressing south in search of better pastures. Hausa agriculturists to the south, turning more bush into millet fields every day, are slowly edging northward. After the harvest in September they welcome cattle to graze in the millet stubble, for manure enriches the land; but if the rains fail and the nomads invade the standing grain, quarrels arise and the farmers invoke the law. And although the government of Niger tries to keep peace and protect both groups, the Bororos mistrust and fear its proceedings.

youth leans comfortably against a staff (above) waiting at a water hole for cattle to drink their fill.

Because they feel insecure, because they fear spirits and intangible powers, the Bororos protect themselves through constant elusiveness. They don't call their children by their real names, which they keep secret, and a son may not bear the name of his father. Many other tabus impose silence upon them. They receive outsiders only with caution. This does not facilitate dealing with them.

Yet I am among them tonight. Leaving the little administrative post of Abalak one morning, I went in search of them with five camels and two settled Fulanis—an interpreter and a cameleer.

My interpreter, Bamo, is a boy about 16 who has just completed grammar school. The cameleer, Abdullah, is ten years older. Although he never went to school he speaks enough French to talk with me; he knows the country and its customs. Both despise the Bororos.

"*Wodaabe,* as we call these people," Bamo told me while we journeyed, "means 'those that one avoids, the unwanted, rejected.' They have a shameful origin—they are children of incest."

Four or five hours later, on the crest of a hill, we reached the first Bororo encampment, encircled by its thorn hedge. Three angry dogs made us unwelcome and the people met us with reserve, but we became friendly in the following days. They belonged to the Godje lineage, rich in cattle but not very good-looking by tribal standards. While with them I met Mokao, a pleasant man in his middle forties, who came visiting; he invited me to go and travel with his family, and I accepted. We found them six hours' march farther on.

Of the handsome Binga'en lineage, "sons of Nga," Mokao's family come much closer to ideal beauty. I can admire them at leisure in the *ruume* dances, study their manners in the routine of camp and trail.

The sound of voices wakes me up at dawn. From my tent I see some old men chatting. Wrapped in blankets and seated on straw mats, near an extinct fire, they are waiting for the sun to chase the chill of the night. At some distance, still adorned for yesterday's dance, a few girls retouch their makeup for the new day. Beyond, among the acacias, couples are stretching, rising from their mats. Young men in leather pants and wide conical hats adorned with ostrich feathers, armed with spears and swords, walk by twos or threes from one group to another.

And the air resounds with interminable salutations. *"Foma, foma? How are you, how are you? And how are your health, your family, your herd? Where are your children? Have you spent a good night, a good week?..."*

"Sago, sago. All is fine, all is fine," the others answer.

"Baraka, baraka. Blessings, blessings."

The long list of polite questions answered, the parts are reversed and it starts again. These greetings are exchanged as if with total indifference, eyes averted in deference and respect.

MOKAO, WHOSE FAMILY is especially likable, greets everybody. His gentle and dignified wife Mama and his pretty daughter Bebe, a girl of 15, help distribute large calabashes of creamy milk to visitors from other households. Mokao serves the men, Mama the women of ripe age, Bebe the young women. When the women have returned to their respective camps to work, the men palaver in the shade of trees. Sometimes one or another moves to a different group, under another tree. And the greetings, endlessly recited in monotone singsong, are followed by many invitations of *"Leste—*sit down."

The morning unwinds from "Foma" to "Foma." The sun climbs irresistibly, making the air as thick as wool and slowing down all activities, then starts its descending course.

By midafternoon the young women have come back and, like the men, sit in groups in the shade of trees which, hung with swords, hats, and rags, look like coat stands. Eventually five or six young men, coming out into the sun, form a circle. Resting nonchalantly against each other, elbows on shoulders, they timidly strike up a song.

A smile of satisfaction on their painted faces, other men detach themselves from the shade and come to join the first, little by little. Their circle bristles with swords that little naked boys caress with respect, and their chant has taken shape. The circle turns, the hands and the feet mark the rhythm; it is again the ruume, the most popular dance.

Foreheads shaved high to enhance their convexity, and all their jewels of brass and copper shining in the late-afternoon sun, the young women come later. They observe the performers with reserve, eyes slightly lowered, some sewing to pretend indifference. However, they bring, carefully folded on their heads, the blankets they will share after the dance with the men of their choice.

Again an old woman derides those dancers whose physiques fail to glorify the race, and old men reprimand the circle for its lack of enthusiasm. Impassive but hurt, the dancers step faster, sing louder. The earth trembles with the beat of the feet and the clapping of their hands tears the air. Their song rises and widens, overwhelming all the other sounds of the savanna, and it seems that nothing exists but the Bororos and their song.

"Fff . . .," sighs Mokao with relief the next morning as he greets me in the lengthy manner of his people. "They're all gone. Now I can give you more milk again." As on other quiet days, he and Mama put down at my feet two immense calabashes which they stabilize by digging a small hole under each. One calabash contains about three gallons of fresh, foaming milk; the other, as much milk from last night on which floats a thick cream. "Milk: drink! Cream: eat! All!" he urges me.

I, who never drink milk at home, absorb milk and cream for breakfast, buttermilk at midmorning after butter has been made, curdled milk in the afternoon, and again fresh milk at night. Now I believe that one can, like the Bororos in this season, feed almost exclusively on this liquid and not go hungry.

Today we are moving. We move every two or three days, and sometimes we stay only one night at a given spot. Sometimes we walk for an hour or more, sometimes we only go over the next dune. Sometimes we move with all our neighbors, sometimes with only a few or none of them. Much excitement rises when Mokao's family travels with the rest of the Binga'en and even the Bikoro'en, "sons of Koro," another lineage. Then with moving herds dotting the whole area the march looks like a real exodus. This happens on certain auspicious days, days of good omen when every Bororo in the Azaouak loads his carrying ox.

Often it is not clear to me why we move. We never seem to leave less grass behind and we leave a relatively clear pool shaded by trees full of singing birds for a dirty puddle. It seems as if the zebus need this movement and the Bororos, like the white cattle egrets, just follow. Abdullah says: "Cows are like people. If you give someone much sauce with his millet, he eats the sauce and leaves the millet. So with the cows: When they have eaten the best grass they want to move on."

Except for Mokao, who goes around socializing, everybody is busy packing. Mama and Goshi, her 18-year-old daughter, dismantle and pack the wooden beds and the little shelter, roll straw mats, wrap calabashes in special straw covers, gather spoons and ladles, mortar and pestle, and wooden bowls. They load a carrying ox and donkeys fetched by Bebe and Kassa, her 13-year-old sister. Kabo, a boy of 11, helps a bit, watching the cattle from the corner of one eye and quick to throw his stick at a straying cow. This is the time — about 10 or 11 a.m. — when the cows come back from pasture to feed their calves, and they must be kept together till time to leave.

While the ox, the donkeys, and a camel are being loaded, Kabo and Bebe start driving the cattle away. Kabo walks in front, a man's sword at his side and his hands resting on a stick laid across his shoulders. He talks to the cattle and calls them, and they follow like well-trained dogs. A cow even comes to his side and licks his hand, then his face. He laughs with pleasure.

The Bororos love their cows; they treat them almost like pets, giving each a name—they sometimes name their children after favorite cattle —and letting them die of old age. They only cull a bad milker or an old bull to pay tax to the *goumiers* (a corps of mounted police composed of Tuareg and a few of the so-called red Fulanis). The sacrificial beast for a wedding or a birth must be of good quality.

Bebe brings up the rear. She watches that no calf strays. With two heavy brass anklets on each leg—which she will not discard until she has borne two children—she cannot run as fast as Kabo.

Once in a while Kabo stops to let the cattle graze. Then, with voice and stick, he gathers them together again and moves on. In a mood for mischief he jumps on the back of a calf and, laughing with all his teeth, spurs it into a trot. Bebe runs after him and pulls him off. Without ill-feeling he resumes his place ahead of the herd and starts improvising a song at the top of his voice: "I walk before my father's cows / They eat grass / Nobody bothers me / And I am happy / When I will be a man / I will also have a herd. . . ."

Now the others have left the camp and a few vultures have taken it over. They may find a little strip of leather. Dung beetles scavenge every trace of dung. Nature loses nothing. Soon grass will hide the ashes of the fire and there will be no sign of the Bororos' passage.

Mounted on a camel, Mokao overtakes the herd and shouts instructions to Kabo. A little later the boy and his sister find Mokao's camel saddle under a tree: the new campsite. Mokao has already disappeared to a new palaver tree. Kabo and Bebe separate the cows from the calves, chasing the former to pasture and taking the latter to drink at the new water hole. The others arrive—Kassa on a donkey, with a baby goat in her lap; Goshi on another donkey, leading the carrying ox; Mama walking behind leading a camel and carrying the day's milk in a calabash on her head. As they unload things near Mokao's saddle, Mama, who does much of the work, goes to fetch water and firewood.

Abdullah, Bamo, and I set up camp nearby at a place designated by Mokao. At first he would indicate a spot a hundred yards from his camp. Since then he had let us come closer until we are as near his hut as his own brother would live.

It is about noon, the temperature of hell. The cows gone and the calves safely in shade, Kabo collapses under a thorny tree, in a blotch of shade generously sprinkled with sunshine. He sleeps, smiling in a dream. Mama and her daughters busy themselves very slowly, starting to put things into place.

Daily, scouts roam the savanna to find new pastures. Every moving day is much the same. We are in *terre salée*, of grasses rich in minerals. We are getting closer, though so little at a time, to In Waggeur,

Garish umbrella shades Bororo men waiting to dance the yakey, *a display of virile elegance. Darkened lips and eyelids emphasize the prized whiteness of their teeth and eyes—physical beauty, like cattle, engrosses the Bororos. Before the* ruume, *the everyday dance of the wet season, men (above) bind tightly rolled cotton cloth around their heads, then insert black ostrich plumes.*

Line of cotton-skirted men stamps to a slow rhythm before harshly critical elders during the annual gathering of the nomadic Bororos. Only
those well-favored in the yakey (far left) dare take part, for in this
gerewol, or festival dance, the old men and women ridicule the slightest
deviation from their standards of beauty: light copper-colored skin, delicate nose and lips, high foreheads, white teeth and eyes. Meanwhile,
the young women of assembled lineages (left) stand watching. They
choose favorites among the men, and perhaps a marriage will result.
Cotton blankets shade their heads, and rows of bracelets circle their arms.
Brass anklets, polished with sand and mud, gleam on their legs;
Bororo women stop wearing them after the birth of their second child.

An outstanding example
of ideal Bororo manhood,
this yakey dancer wears
cowrie shells and metal
beads in strands dan-
gling from a band under
his cotton headdress. He
stands tall and proud,
confident of pleasing a
beautiful young woman.
The one above has thread-
ed her long hair through
the polished brass spools
hanging down her back.

a long chain of ponds flowing into each other during the rains but almost vanishing during the driest months. They lie in a large valley some
80 miles northeast as the crow flies. Mokao's people started their migration almost that far to the southeast, but since their pastoral needs
lead them along a roundabout zigzagging way, they cover much greater
distances. The cattle must be kept in the best possible condition.

I cannot estimate their numbers. A Bororo rarely confides such matters; for me to try to count a herd would give offense.

Before I joined Mokao, I had some difficulty with the Godje because
of the cattle's shyness—they started a stampede as soon as they saw me
or caught my scent, and this made the Godje impatient with my presence. Mokao's zebus, on the contrary, are quite tame. They would eat
my tent if I let them—their urge for salt makes them lick anything I
leave around. His dogs are just as sociable. "Animals are like their
masters," he explains.

Mokao himself is a sophisticated man by Bororo standards. He often
wears cotton robes over his leather pants; and through intelligence,
cunning, and broadmindedness—perhaps also through the prestige of
relative wealth—he imposes himself upon his peers and gets along
well with people of other groups, even the Tuareg, traditionally at
daggers drawn with the Bororos.

Though Mokao may disappear in the bush with another woman
after a long evening dance, he is monogamous. This is not the case
with every Bororo. His eldest brother has three wives. Each has a hut
of her own, as does his widowed mother, who lives with them.

Reticence surrounds family matters, such as Goshi's pregnancy.
Perhaps she has left her husband to bear her first child with her mother's help, according to custom; perhaps she is unmarried. The Bororos'
morals offer much scope to their neighbors' sarcasm, though no young
woman wanders to a market unescorted.

But the Bororos have their own concepts of honor. They do not call
for help when attacked by hyena or man but fight courageously alone;
they disdain any admission of hunger or thirst; they will not eat or
drink before in-laws, or even name them; they do not laugh loudly and
they hide pain. . . . What they call "shame" strangely resembles pride.

As the shadows grow longer, life stirs again in Mokao's camp. Mama
and Goshi set up a stand and arrange the many calabashes on it by
order of size. Later, while Goshi milks the cows, Mama starts building
a shelter of limber branches and matting.

Following Bororo tradition, the camp conforms to a rigid pattern.
A daangol, or calf-rope, running north-south along the entrance, sep-
arates the husband's area—the cattle corral—from the wife's, which is
enclosed by a hedge of thorny branches opening to the west. In the
rear of the wife's area is her calabash stand; there are two beds, one
sheltered by the small hut; in front is her fire. The hut, no larger than
Mama's bed, is only set up during the weeks of rain. The other bed
receives the three daughters, and Kabo sleeps on a mat on the ground;
the children pull mats over their heads when it rains.

Almost invariably, I can tell what is happening in the camp by the height of the sun. After the first milking, at daybreak, Goshi makes butter by beating milk with a wooden whisk, then shaking it in a container made of two tightly fitting calabashes, rather like a cocktail shaker. Meanwhile Kassa, riding a donkey, goes to the pond to fill a goatskin with water. When the cattle have finished chewing the cud, they drink; Kabo takes them for water if the pond is far off. By eleven o'clock when the cows are back to feed their calves, there are generally a few visitors around.

Women—cousins, in-laws, or friends of Mama and her daughters—sit in the shade of a tree and sew, weave a mat, carve designs in a calabash, or braid hair. Under another tree, on the corral side, men talk of cattle—naturally. They have few handicrafts, and buy almost everything they need from the settled folk.

Children play. Like children around the world they imitate their elders. Little girls shape small calabashes out of clay. They fill them with sand, which they imagine to be milk, and cover them with pieces of old mats to keep out flies and trash. Little boys use clay to fashion cows. They peel and carve twigs to give them the color and shape of zebu horns. They dig little wells. Like men, they dance and chant. But always they remember their duties—if calves get to the cows to suck between feeding times, and rob the family of a milking, the children are to blame.

Boys begin watching the herds at the age of six or seven. Many spend their days with flocks of sheep and goats but, except for Kassa's pet kid, this family has none. Abdullah scorns this, for people, he says, should have animals to slaughter to honor guests.

Often I lounge in the shade of my own tree, only half awake in the torpor of noon and hardly able to gather more energy than I need to move with the shade. Abdullah and Bamo slumber much of the time. Mokao frequently sits with us. Every day he asks for a magazine of mine to see a photograph of a Lebanese policeman with a red cap and an enormous lyre-shaped mustache. And every day he asks me whether this man has horns like a bull's under his nose. Then he snaps his fingers, shakes his head in disbelief, and gestures that he would flee if this strange creature ever came his way.

Sometimes a Tuareg passes by and stops to enjoy hospitality. He invariably says that he is looking for a lost cow, yet loses half a day or more drinking milk at the Bororos' expense. I suspect that these men do not even own cows. Yet Bororos and Tuareg often fight bloody battles around wells; when swords are drawn, they sever hands or feet with single blows.

The Tuareg are not alone in taking advantage of the Bororos. Other Fulanis—who call themselves "red," *bodejo,* a term used also for Europeans—will do as much. But the Bororos resent most bitterly the goumiers, who collect taxes from nomads.

A dozen of them once passed through Mokao's encampment while I was there. They wore magnificent robes and uniform boots of red leather; they were armed to the teeth and mounted on frisky horses. They stopped in the next valley and started rounding up cows.

Resting through the heat of afternoon, Mokao's son Kabo leans against his maternal uncle Dadji. Leather pouches hold amulets to ward off harm. Both Mokao and Dadji will give Kabo cattle to start a herd when he marries. Loath to sell a single cow, Bororos cherish their herds as legacies for future generations.

Following Mokao, who had gone on their heels to try to arrange matters, I saw dozens of Bororos rushing from every point of the savanna with spears, swords, bows and arrows. They were in a mad rage, these pleasant people; their eyes were bloodshot and they meant to use their weapons. They started encircling the horsemen. The latter fired warning shots over their heads, attracting even more enemies. But Mokao kept shuttling between the groups, preaching calm. He finally reached a compromise with the goumiers and only a few animals were taken.

Though Bororos pay taxes—I have seen papers for sums as high as $500—and understand justice, they lack understanding of official procedures. And, totally against all government policy, a nurse at a bush clinic might turn a Bororo away. Uneducated—they refuse to go to school—they have no representatives of their own.

To dance practically every day and to be beautiful seems their dominant concern during the rainy season. Usually they dance the ruume. Sometimes, however, standing in a row instead of a circle, they dance the *yakey*, in which they utter kisslike sounds while showing the whiteness of their teeth and eyeballs in strange grimaces.

At sunset, Mokao or Kabo lights a fire in the corral for the cattle and, one after the other, the cows come and take their places around it for the night. The smoke may deter insects—or hyenas. The cows are milked once more. When the last animal has stopped lowing, children can still be heard running and screaming for a while. Then the insects start their concert.

Except where scattered acacias, like inkspots, blotch it out, the savanna gleams under a crescent of moon; and red embers, like a wound of the night, shine through the legs of the cattle. Fragments of a chant hover in the distance. During the season of dances, it is said, when every man is more handsome than the next, many a wife runs away with a lover, never to return.

The grass, now knee-high, has lost the acidity of its green and rains have become less frequent. The word *gerewol* is on all lips and, to prepare for this great festival which will reunite the nomads, Mokao leaves one morning on camelback for the market of Kao to buy new clothes for himself and his family. He drives before him a cow to sell. Back after seven days, he learns that his second camel has been stolen and he sets out to try to find it. Another seven days go by, but he reappears with his lost animal. And he tells us how, day after day, for more than 65 miles, he has patiently read the sand and isolated his camel's tracks among a hundred. He found his camel grazing among others—but not the thief.

From pond to pond the Bororos have finally reached In Waggeur. It is September and rains have become so rare that Mama does not set up the little hut. Kassa's kid has become a goat and Goshi has given birth to a beautiful little boy.

The Bororos are all over the valley, and the dance of the gerewol begins. Spectators stand watching with men to the right, women to the left. Few are the dancers, for only the most handsome dare face the critics, particularly harsh now. *(Continued on page 194)*

Muffled thuds carry across the savanna as women (opposite) pound sorghum. Bororos regard food preparation as strictly women's work. A married woman (left) pours millet into milk in one of the large calabashes arranged according to tradition on her stand. As cattle bring the husband status, so calabashes confirm the matron's position in society. While men tend the herds, women concern themselves with the milk; they may keep the money from any excess they sell. Milking and other household chores finished, Mama and her daughter Bebe (below) set up the frame of her hut. Piles of reed and straw mats will cushion Mama's bed.

Following the herd in the lifelong quest for grass and water, Mokao's 13-year-old daughter Kassa cradles a young kid. Every few days the family moves to fresh pastures, for during these rainy weeks of summer the animals must build strength for the dry months of withered grass to come. Other tribes admire the Bororos as masters of stock breeding, for their cattle possess great endurance as well as good milk-producing ability. Below, Mama carries milk in a calabash on her head as she leads a camel; Goshi and Kassa follow on donkeys. Dadji leads, for Mokao has gone to market to buy finery for the coming reunion.

Hour after hour, from early afternoon until sunset, chants succeed chants. An old woman, pulling a pack saddle at the end of a rope, threatens to put it on the back of any dancer who does not meet the standards. The young men stamp to a slow rhythm. Through the red paste on their faces seep droplets of sweat. They dance, erect and noble, without betraying their fatigue.

At the end of the afternoon, three girls, chosen by the old people for their beauty, approach with a slow and grave dignity. They kneel midway between the dancers and the spectators, facing the former with eyes lowered. There they remain until an old man helps them to rise, one by one. Then, walking slowly and majestically, arms swinging high, they go up to the dancers and each discreetly indicates the man of her choice before returning to her place.

When the last girl has done this the dance ends abruptly and, in great tumult, the crowd moves a little farther to where other young men have started a yakey. Stopping only to gorge themselves with milk brought in large calabashes by young women, they will dance— the ruume this time—until late into the night.

While the rituals of the dance continue, the older men of each lineage convene for their yearly *wurso*, discussions of affairs of common interest. Marriages arranged in childhood are celebrated now with offerings of cattle. Now the young husband whose wife has borne a child is free to take his cattle from his father's care; a new household is complete. Perhaps a family has lost its herd to famine or disease; now the patrilineal kin make *nanga na'i*, loans of healthy stock, so that life may go on as it should.

Celebrations over, distributions of cattle established, the nomads will scatter and start walking south again. Yet first, in Mokao's camp, there will be one more feast, for he will sacrifice two cows in honor of Goshi's little son and there will be many guests.

Now insects and the eager teeth of camels have undressed the trees and bared the long bony thorns, warning of cruel days ahead. The songs of men and frogs have died, replaced by the creaking of pulleys at the wells. Nights have grown cold and the children cough painfully, huddled under straw mats. Nobody lingers anymore under the palaver trees. Every two days Mokao takes his herd to a well and draws great quantities of water for the cattle. Other days are spent on ever more distant pastures. As for Mama, she often walks considerable distances to barter milk for millet, or even millet bran, in the villages.

By January or February, when water and grass will have become utterly rare, tribes and families will have dispersed for survival and the sole concern of everyone will be to stay alive and keep the herds alive until the rains. Then one day, in May or June, all the cows will turn their heads to the northeast and the Bororos will know the rains have come—somewhere at least. And a song will rise again to the sky.

With the nomads scattered far, I bid farewell to my friends.

"The wet and the dry season will come back again and again," Mokao tells me, holding my hands in his, "but they will never alter my friendship for you."

Bororo goatherds make their way home to camp as the sun slips toward
the acacia trees on the skyline. As the boys dawdle along, they talk of
the important things: the dry months about to begin; the dancing sure to
take place that night; new clothes and bright beads; and the great herds
of zebu cattle each will possess, bringing prosperity and happiness.

Index

Illustrations and illustrations references appear in *italics*.

Acknowledgments

The Special Publications Division is grateful to the authorities listed here for their generous cooperation and assistance during the preparation of this book:

Michael M. Ameen, Jr., Joseph R. Applegate, Richard L. Berkowitz, G. D. Berreman, Marguerite Dupire, C. Edward Hopen, Michael M. Horowitz, Ronald J. Maduro, Johannes Nicolaisen, Jordan K. Ngubane, George Rentz, Henry B. Roberts, Benson Saler, Richard Salzer, Clifford A. Sather, Henry W. Setzer, Louise Sweet, George Watson.

Additional References

For additional reading, you may wish to obtain the Special Publications *Gypsies* and *Vanishing Peoples of the Earth*, to consult the *National Geographic Index* for related articles, and to refer to the following books:

Paul Bohannan and George Dalton, eds., *Markets in Africa*; Cottie Burland, *Men Without Machines*; J. L. Cloudsley-Thompson and M. J. Chadwick, *Life in Deserts*; Ian George Cunnison, *Nomads and the Nineteen-Sixties*; H. R. P. Dickson, *The Arab of the Desert*; Neville Dyson-Hudson, *Karimojong Politics*; Henry Field, *Contributions to the Anthropology of Iran*; J. H. Jager Gerlings, *Problems of Nomadism*.

Allan R. Holmberg, *Nomads of the Long Bow*; C. Edward Hopen, *The Pastoral Fulbe Family in Gwandu*; Douglas L. Johnson, *The Nature of Nomadism*; Harold Lamb, *The Earth Shakers*; Owen Lattimore, *Nomads and Commissars*; Johannes Nicolaisen, *The Ecology and Culture of the Pastoral Tuareg*; A. T. Olmstead, *The History of the Persian Empire*; H. St. John B. Philby, *The Empty Quarter*; Carl R. Raswan, *Black Tents of Arabia*.

George Rentz, *A Sketch of the Geography, People and History of the Arabian Peninsula*; John E. Rouse, *World Cattle*; Satya Pal Ruhela, *The Gaduliya Lohars of Rajasthan*; Marshall D. Sahlins, *The Tribesmen*; F. W. de St. Croix, *The Fulani of Northern Nigeria*; Richard H. Sanger, *The Arabian Peninsula*; Knut Schmidt-Nielsen, *Desert Animals*; Elman R. Service, *The Hunters*.

David E. Sopher, *The Sea Nomads*; Paul Spencer, *The Samburu*; Derrick J. Stenning, *Savannah Nomads*; Sir Percy Sykes, *A History of Persia*; Wilfred Thesiger, *Arabian Sands*; Elizabeth Marshall Thomas, *The Harmless People*; James Tod, *Annals and Antiquities of Rajasthan*; Colin M. Turnbull, *The Forest People* and *Wayward Servants*; Marie-Thérèse Ullens de Schooten, *Lords of the Mountains*; UNESCO, *Paris Symposium of the Problems of the Arid Zone, 1960*; Frederick L. Wernstedt and J. E. Spencer, *The Philippine Island World*; Donald N. Wilber, *Contemporary Iran*.

Composition for Nomads of the World by National Geographic's Phototypographic
Division, John E. McConnell, Manager. Printed and bound by Fawcett Printing Corp.,
Rockville, Md. Color separations by Colorgraphics, Inc., Beltsville, Md.; Graphic Color
Plate, Inc., Stamford, Conn.; The Lanman Company, Alexandria, Va.; Lebanon Valley
Offset Company, Inc., Annville, Pa.; and Progressive Color Corp., Rockville, Md. Dust
jacket printed by Case Hoyt, Rochester, N.Y.

NATIONAL GEOGRAPHIC SOCIETY

WASHINGTON, D. C.

Organized "for the increase and diffusion of geographic knowledge"

GILBERT HOVEY GROSVENOR
Editor, 1899-1954; President, 1920-1954
Chairman of the Board, 1954-1966

THE NATIONAL GEOGRAPHIC SOCIETY is chartered in Washington, D. C., in accordance with the laws of the United States, as a nonprofit scientific and educational organization for increasing and diffusing geographic knowledge and promoting research and exploration. Since 1890 the Society has supported 723 explorations and research projects, adding immeasurably to man's knowledge of earth, sea, and sky. It diffuses this knowledge through its monthly journal, NATIONAL GEOGRAPHIC; more than 27 million maps distributed each year; its books, globes, atlases, and filmstrips; 30 School Bulletins a year in color; information services to press, radio, and television; technical reports; exhibits from around the world in Explorers Hall; and a nationwide series of programs on television.
Articles and photographs of travel, natural history, and expeditions to far places are desired. For material used, generous remuneration is made.

MELVIN M. PAYNE, President
ROBERT E. DOYLE, Vice President and Secretary
LEONARD CARMICHAEL, Vice President for Research and Exploration
GILBERT M. GROSVENOR, Vice President
THOMAS M. BEERS, Vice President and Associate Secretary
HILLEARY F. HOSKINSON, Treasurer
OWEN R. ANDERSON, WILLIAM T. BELL,
LEONARD J. GRANT, W. EDWARD ROSCHER,
C. VERNON SANDERS, Associate Secretaries

BOARD OF TRUSTEES
MELVILLE BELL GROSVENOR
Chairman of the Board and Editor-in-Chief
THOMAS W. McKNEW, Advisory Chairman of the Board

LEONARD CARMICHAEL, Former
Secretary, Smithsonian Institution
LLOYD H. ELLIOTT, President,
George Washington University
CRAWFORD H. GREENEWALT
Chairman, Finance Committee,
E. I. du Pont de Nemours & Company
GILBERT M. GROSVENOR
Editor, National Geographic
ARTHUR B. HANSON, General
Counsel, National Geographic Society
CARYL P. HASKINS, Former
President, Carnegie Institution
of Washington
EMORY S. LAND, Vice Admiral,
U. S. Navy (Ret.), Former President,
Air Transport Association
CURTIS E. LeMAY, Former Chief
of Staff, U. S. Air Force
H. RANDOLPH MADDOX
Former Vice President, American
Telephone & Telegraph Company
WM. McCHESNEY MARTIN, JR.
Former Chairman, Board of
Governors, Federal Reserve System
BENJAMIN M. McKELWAY
Editorial Chairman, Washington Star

MELVIN M. PAYNE, President,
National Geographic Society
LAURANCE S. ROCKEFELLER
President, Rockefeller Brothers Fund
ROBERT C. SEAMANS, JR.
Secretary of the Air Force
JUAN T. TRIPPE, Honorary
Chairman of the Board,
Pan American World Airways
FREDERICK G. VOSBURGH
Former Editor, National Geographic
JAMES H. WAKELIN, JR.
Assistant Secretary of Commerce
for Science and Technology
EARL WARREN, Former
Chief Justice of the United States
JAMES E. WEBB, Former
Administrator, National Aeronautics
and Space Administration
ALEXANDER WETMORE
Research Associate,
Smithsonian Institution
LLOYD B. WILSON (Emeritus)
Honorary Board Chairman,
Chesapeake & Potomac
Telephone Company
CONRAD L. WIRTH, Former
Director, National Park Service

LOUIS B. WRIGHT, Former Director,
Folger Shakespeare Library

COMMITTEE FOR RESEARCH AND EXPLORATION
LEONARD CARMICHAEL, Chairman
ALEXANDER WETMORE and MELVIN M. PAYNE, Vice Chairmen
GILBERT M. GROSVENOR, MELVILLE BELL GROSVENOR,
CARYL P. HASKINS, EMORY S. LAND, THOMAS W. McKNEW, T.
DALE STEWART, Physical Anthropologist Emeritus, Smithsonian Institution, MATTHEW W. STIRLING, Research Associate, Smithsonian Institution, JAMES H. WAKELIN, JR., FRANK C. WHITMORE, JR., Research Geologist, U. S. Geological Survey, CONRAD L. WIRTH, FREDERICK G. VOSBURGH, and PAUL A. ZAHL; BARRY C. BISHOP, Secretary on leave;
EDWIN W. SNIDER, Secretary

Assistant Secretaries of the Society:
EVERETT C. BROWN, FRANK S. DELK, JOSEPH B. HOGAN,
RAYMOND T. McELLIGOTT, JR., EDWIN W. SNIDER
Assistant Treasurer: WARD S. PHELPS

Leonard J. Grant, Editorial Assistant to the President; Edwin W. Snider, Richard E. Pearson, Administrative Assistants to the President; Judith N. Dixon, Administrative Assistant to the Chairman and Editor-in-Chief; Lenore W. Kessler, Administrative Assistant to the Advisory Chairman of the Board

SECRETARY'S STAFF: *Administrative:* Earl Corliss, Jr., Harriet Carey, Frederick C. Gale. *Accounting:* Jay H. Givans, George F. Fogle, Alfred J. Hayre, William G. McGhee, Martha Allen Baggett. *Statistics:* Thomas M. Kent. *Payroll and Retirement:* Howard R. Hudson (Supervisor); Mary L. Whitmore, Dorothy L. Dameron (Assistants). *Procurement:* J. P. M. Johnston, Thomas L. Fletcher, Robert G. Corey, Sheila H. Immel. *Membership Research:* Charles T. Kneeland. *Membership Fulfillment:* Geneva S. Robinson, Paul B. Tylor, Peter F. Woods. *Computer Center:* Lewis P. Lowe. *Promotion:* Robert J. Warfel, Towne Windom, John S. Shilgalis. *Printing:* Joe M. Barlett, Frank S. Oliverio. *Production Control:* James P. Kelly. *Personnel:* James B. Mahon, Adrian L. Loftin, Jr., Glenn G. Pepperman, Nellie E. Sinclair. *Medical:* Thomas L. Hartman, M. D. *Translation:* Zbigniew Jan Lutyk

NATIONAL GEOGRAPHIC MAGAZINE

MELVILLE BELL GROSVENOR Editor-in-Chief and Board Chairman
MELVIN M. PAYNE President of the Society

GILBERT M. GROSVENOR Editor

FRANC SHOR, JOHN SCOFIELD Associate Editors

Senior Assistant Editors
Allan C. Fisher, Jr., Kenneth MacLeish, Robert L. Conly, W. E. Garrett

Assistant Editors: Jules B. Billard, Andrew H. Brown, James Cerruti, Edward J. Linehan, Carolyn Bennett Patterson, Howell Walker, Kenneth F. Weaver
Senior Editorial Staff: William S. Ellis, Rowe Findley, William Graves, Jay Johnston, Robert P. Jordan, Joseph Judge, Nathaniel T. Kenney, Samuel W. Matthews, Bart McDowell; Senior Scientist: Paul A. Zahl
Foreign Editorial Staff: Luis Marden (Chief); Thomas J. Abercrombie, Howard La Fay, Volkmar Wentzel, Peter T. White
Editorial Staff: Harvey Arden, Thomas Y. Canby, Louis de la Haba, Mike W. Edwards, Noel Grove, Alice J. Hall, Werner Janney, Jerry Kline, John L. McIntosh, Elizabeth A. Moize, Ethel A. Starbird, Gordon Young
Editorial Layout: Howard E. Paine (Chief); Charles C. Uhl, John M. Lavery
Geographic Art: William N. Palmstrom (Chief). *Artists:* Peter V. Bianchi, Lisa Biganzoli, William H. Bond, John W. Lothers, Robert C. Magis, Robert W. Nicholson, Ned M. Seidler. *Cartographic Artists:* Victor J. Kelley, Snejinka Stefanoff. *Research:* Walter Q. Crowe (Supervisor); Virginia L. Baza, George W. Beatty, John D. Garst, Jean B. McConville, Dorothy A. Nicholson, Isaac Ortiz (Production). Marie L. Barnes (Administrative Assistant)
Editorial Research: Margaret G. Bledsoe (Chief); Ann K. Wendt (Associate Chief), Alice M. Bowsher, Jan Holderness, Levenia Loder, Frances H. Parker
Geographic Research: George Crossette (Chief); Newton V. Blakeslee (Assistant Chief), Leon J. Canova, Bette Joan Goss, Lesley B. Lane, John A. Weeks
Phototypography: John E. McConnell (Chief); Lawrence F. Ludwig (Assistant Chief)
Library: Virginia Carter Hills (Librarian); Melba Barnes, Louise A. Robinson, Esther Ann Manion (Librarian Emeritus)
Editorial Administration: Joyce W. McKean, Assistant to the Editor; Virginia H. Finnegan, Winifred M. Myers, Shirley Neff, Inez D. Wilkinson (Editorial Assistants); Dorothy M. Corson (Indexes); Rosalie K. Millerd, Lorine Wendling (Files); Evelyn Fox, Dolores Kennedy (Transportation); Carolyn F. Clewell (Correspondence); Jeanne S. Duiker (Archives)
ILLUSTRATIONS STAFF: *Illustrations Editor:* Herbert S. Wilburn, Jr. *Associate Illustrations Editor:* Thomas R. Smith. *Art Editor:* Andrew Poggenpohl. *Assistant Illustrations Editors:* Mary S. Griswold, O. Louis Mazzatenta, Charlene Murphy, Robert S. Patton. *Layout and Production:* H. Edward Kim (Chief). *Picture Editors:* David L. Arnold, Michael E. Long, Elie S. Rogers, W. Allan Royce, Jon Schneeberger, C. William Snead. *Research:* Paula C. Simmons. Barbara A. Shattuck (Asst.). *Librarian:* L. Fern Dame
Engraving and Printing: Dee J. Andella (Chief); John R. Metcalfe, William W. Smith, James R. Whitney
PHOTOGRAPHIC STAFF: *Director of Photography:* Robert E. Gilka. *Assistant Director:* Dean Conger. *Film Review:* Albert Moldvay (Chief); Guy W. Starling (Assistant Chief). *Photographic Equipment:* John E. Fletcher (Chief), Donald McBain. *Pictorial Research:* Walter Meayers Edwards (Chief). *Photographers:* James L. Amos, James P. Blair, Bruce Dale, Dick Durrance II, Otis Imboden, Emory Kristof, Bates Littlehales, George F. Mobley, Robert S. Oakes, Winfield Parks, Joseph J. Scherschel, Robert F. Sisson, James L. Stanfield. Lilian Davidson (Administration). *Photographic Laboratories:* Carl M. Shrader (Chief); Milton A. Ford (Associate Chief); Herbert Altemus, Jr., David H. Chisman, Claude E. Petrone, Donald E. Stemper

RELATED EDUCATIONAL SERVICES OF THE SOCIETY
Cartography: William T. Peele (Chief); David W. Cook (Assistant Chief). *Cartographic Staff:* Margery K. Barkdull, Charles F. Case, Ted Dachtera, Richard J. Darley, John F. Dorr, Russel G. Fritz, Richard R. Furno, Charles W. Gotthardt, Jr., Catherine M. Hart, Donald A. Jaeger, Harry D. Kauhane, James W. Killion, Manuela G. Kogutowicz, Charles L. Miller, David L. Moore, Robert W. Northrop, Richard K. Rogers, John F. Shupe, Charles L. Stern, Douglas A. Strobel, George E. Stuart (Archeology), Tibor G. Toth, Thomas A. Wall, Thomas A. Walsh
Books: Merle Severy (Chief); Seymour L. Fishbein (Assistant Chief), Thomas B. Allen, Ross Bennett, Charles O. Hyman, Anne Dirkes Kobor, John J. Putman, David F. Robinson, Verla Lee Smith
Special Publications: Robert L. Breeden (Chief); Donald J. Crump (Asst. Chief), Josephine B. Bolt, David R. Bridge, Linda Bridge, Margery G. Dunn, Johanna G. Farren, Ronald Fisher, Mary Ann Harrell, Bryan Hodgson, Geraldine Linder, Robert Messer, Cynthia Ramsay, Philip B. Silcott, Joseph A. Taney
School Service: Ralph Gray (Chief and Editor of National Geographic School Bulletin); Arthur P. Miller, Jr. (Assistant Chief and Associate Editor of School Bulletin). Joseph B. Goodwin, Ellen Joan Hurst, Paul F. Moize, Charles H. Sloan, Janis Knudsen Wheat. *Educational Filmstrips:* David S. Boyer (Chief); Margaret McKelway Johnson
News Service: Windsor P. Booth (Chief); Paul Sampson (Assistant Chief), Donald J. Frederick, William J. O'Neill, Robert C. Radcliffe; Isabel Clarke
Television: Robert C. Doyle (Chief); David Cooper, Carl W. Harmon, Jr., Sidney Platt, Patricia F. Northrop (Administrative Assistant)
Lectures: Joanne M. Hess (Chief); Robert G. Fleegal, Mary W. McKinney, Gerald L. Wiley
Explorers Hall: T. Keilor Bentley (Curator-Director)
EUROPEAN OFFICES: W. Edward Roscher (Associate Secretary and Director), Jennifer Moseley (Assistant), 4 Curzon Place, Mayfair, London, W1Y 8EN, England; Jacques Ostier, 6 rue des Petits-Pères, 75-Paris 2e, France
ADVERTISING: *Director:* William A. Boeger, Jr. *National Advertising Manager:* William Turgeon, 630 Fifth Ave., New York, N.Y. 10020. *Regional managers—Eastern:* George W. Kellner, New York. *Midwestern:* Robert R. Henn, Chicago. *Western:* Thomas Martz, San Francisco. *Los Angeles:* Jack Wallace. *Canada:* Robert W. Horan, New York. *Automotive:* John F. Grant, New York. *Travel:* Gerald A. Van Splinter, New York. *International Director:* James L. Till, New York. *European Director:* Richard V. Macy, 21 rue Jean-Mermoz, Paris 8e, France. *Production:* E. M. Pusey, Jr.

Da OCT 1 1 72